I0188061

The Ready Woman

How to Bounce Back from Adversity, Redesign Your Life for Amazing Love & Real Happiness in 9 Steps

By Nekisha Michelle Kee, MSW

Published By Ready Woman Publishing & Media

First Edition

Cover Art: Nia Nicole Usher

Book Layout Team: Amber Allen & Boyo Agboola

Cover photo: Kalvin Reeves – www.kalvinreeves.com

Wardrobe: Fashion to Figure – www.fashiontofigure.com

Edited in part by Erica Walters, Felisha Robinson and Patrina Hughes

ISBN-13: 978-0-9707175-7-4

ISBN-10: 0-9707175-0-4

Table of Contents

Acknowledgements

I want to thank God for giving me the grace, spirit, and courage to tell my story with the respect that it enlightens, strengthens and transforms every soul who dares to read and complete the actions steps necessary to foster lasting change. I take nothing for granted especially not my life. I want to thank my editors Felisha and Erica for the late nights and early mornings and making my words, make sense. I miss you guys, but I am so grateful for your labor of love. I want to thank my intern NIA USHER for articulating a fantastic book cover graphically. You have been such a joy and sweetheart to work with.

I want to thank my mentor, friend and spiritual sister Patrina Hughes who always has a kind word, good coaching and good sarcasm for me. Eighteen years and it still seems like it was yesterday when we discovered each other at church. I want to thank Dr. Christine H. Diggs for writing my foreword, and always being a phone call or text message away when I need help, a mother's love, and supportive guidance. Since college, you have been steering me straight and one of my biggest cheerleaders.

Dr. Valda Hilton is more than a spiritual mother; she is my friend, my light, and my moral compass. Thank you for looking after me, laughing with me, teaching me, modeling before me and most of all loving me when I didn't know how to love myself.

I want to thank every client that allowed me to test out my theories and intuitive hunches in our sessions. The Ready Woman worked for me, and when I saw it working for you guys, I knew it was time to share it with the world.

I am so appreciative for my former life coach actress and healthy lifestyle advocate AJ Johnson, your strength, words and focus allowed me to believe in me and understand the discipline to have the life I want. Our time together was so priceless.

My girl Okera Banks, thank you for teaching me to have thick skin and focus on my business. Your swag is to die for, and I love how you keep me looking great for your clothing collection. I own my curves and cuteness because of you.

To Crystal Washington Martin who is my inspiration, sounding board, cheerleader, friend, my sissy and an all-around successful class act with a whole lot of sass. The days of the mastermind sitting in our living rooms trying to figure it all out. In the words of DRAKE we started from the bottom, and now we're HERE!!!

Madeline "Maddy" Figueroa Jones editor of Plus Model Magazine. You took me under your wing and pushed me off the ledge and gave me all the inspiration to spread my wings and fly. Thank you for re-discovering my gifts and talents. Thank you for using your platform to help me build my own. Thank you for sharing Ms. Myrna with me. She is a rare jewel, and I am in great company here in Atlanta.

The women who collaborated with me in the sequel to this book called "Diary of a Ready Woman" and especially my girl Amber Allen. Working with you and growing this fantastic project has been a lifesaver. I am so appreciative of your patience and support.

To my success mentor and partner in crime, Angela "AJ" Thompson. Girl, your love is so thick and so full, I have never experienced such a giving person with a big heart as you. I want to be like you when I grow up.

Longtime friend and mentor, Debrena Jackson Gandy, you have been and continue to be a remarkable rare jewel that helps me stay true to me and what I love and be juicy about it. Thank you for nearly 20 years of companionship. Thank you for pulling me into the world of entrepreneurship, women's work and coaching.

My childhood friend Aniko Peeks Williams, you have been ride or die since we were 11 years old and it overjoyed my heart to see that you have supported me in most of my endeavors, been a good listener, and probably the only person on earth that has all of the books I attempted. That is true love and such a friendship, and I don't take lightly. May God continue to grow you and bless you and your family.

To Ursula Stewart & Phillip Stigger, my high school buddies and friends forever, we've been through some things, but we are still here doing our job. I love you guys to life.

My WEWORK buddies and mastermind Sista-friends, Karla Beedles, Candice Ledbetter, Simone Kirlew, Amyr Heard and Kimberly Bennett. You ladies are a breath of fresh air, and your professionalism and expertise continue to propel me forward while blowing me away. Thank you all for being my guardian angels and business confidants.

To my late father, thank you for the good and the ugly, thanks for watching over me and shining your love from heaven. To my late great grand-parents, Nana and Granddaddy, my success is your legacy, and I am so glad you gave me the best 12 years of love, discipline, and God. To my late grandmother, Momma Maggie - you believed in me, and that alone is enough to fuel me for my lifetime. Even when I get tired, I think of what you accomplished with so little. I have no excuse but to be great.

To my grandparents, mother, brothers, uncle, aunt, cousins and others, thank you for life, thank you for every experience, thank you for your unconditional love and thank you for allowing me the freedom to tell my story in my way. It doesn't always feel good, but all things work together for God's greater good. I love you!

Dedication

This book I dedicate to the most loving, sexiest, sweetest, humblest, funniest man I know. My husband, friend, and soulmate Abdulwasiu "Alboyo" Agboola my Nigerian King. I also dedicate this book to my daughters Ciera "Ce Ce" & Islamyaat "Izzy." You two have challenged me to be the best person I can be for you. I love my girls. The road has not been easy but we are healthy, happy, prospering and the best is yet to come.

Foreword

Have you ever been stuck in the ashes of life, unable to move, process, and/or decipher your "here and now" existence much less your life's purpose.... you're just stuck! All you wanted to do was not only get under the bedcovers with pillows over your head but get under the bed itself! Or wish a black hole would just open up and swallow you up...just take you away? Sometimes contemplating your situation takes too much mental and physical energy. And sometimes just not doing anything is too much!

As you reflect over your life and think about what you've been through, how did you make it? What are your current struggles threatening your inner peace? What does your future feel or look like? It's about gut instinct, internal fortitude, unwavering faith, and trust in God to bring you through. But how do you keep the faith when you don't understand the why's of what you're going through? How do you continue to trust when you've heard about a Creator but you don't know or have a personal relationship with your Creator or His ability to subject you to different challenges for the purpose to strengthen you, to guide you towards Heaven?

Romans 8:28 states 'and we know that all things work together for good to them that love God, to them who are the called according to His purpose. James 1: 2 further calls us to <u>*Count it all Joy*</u> when you fall into various trials knowing that the testing of your faith produces patience. It's not a matter of 'if' we will face severe challenges but 'when' we do. James exhorts us to go to God for help to make it through each trial.

I met Nekisha Kee over 20 years ago when she was one of my graduating students in social work at Virginia State University. I had come aboard Virginia State University to take the helm of the Department of Social Work undergoing critical accreditation dilemmas - evaluators citing serious faculty divisiveness, curriculum deficits, lack of university supports and on and on.

I was both her faculty advisor and professor in her last semester. While in the research course as well as her internship, I took note of this very bubbly personality who was truly gifted in both her oratory and writing skills but was marginally living up to that potential. She was certainly an honors student but only producing enough for the bottom rung of honors. She had a beautiful little girl, was a full-time student, living off scholarships, in the talent search program (for first generational college students), sorority, and many more organizations on and off campus. But one day she crashed outside the steps of the social work building, literally passing out on the grounds...and I was there.

Pieces of her background emerged as we talked and talked and talked. Nekisha remembers so much more about how I've impacted her life and she talks of the many life inspirations I've shared with her. Throughout the years and I'm not clear when it happened, the relationship became much more than professor to student, or mentor to mentee. Maybe 'mama bird' as I was affectionately called fueled this relationship.

However, it was not until Nekisha called and said "Dr. Diggs, I wrote a book and had it published." I want you to read it. And read it I did with much agony because I had no idea of the amount of pain, the thoroughness of the rejection she had experienced. The betrayal, the backlash of her parents, the naysayers in her life, nor the will of Nekisha to take her own life was ever evidenced. Yes, I did know that she was raped at thirteen which resulted in her little girl - but not the multiple rapes as recorded in her initial book, The Lord is my Shepherd.

Even as I write this foreword, the lyrics of Kurt Carr's melody God's mercy kept me so I wouldn't let go keeps emerging as I remember God keeps us even when we don't know we need to be kept. 'I just recently reminded Nekisha of Psalm 139:14 which states we are wonderfully and fearfully made….and each of our journeys is unique and made just for each of us. Nekisha's life is a testimony which had to happen so that she could be a blessing to others and lead them out of the wilderness of the pit to becoming empowered and walking into their purpose divinely designed by God.

Nekisha Kee has again produced a raw, real, and relatable life expose' which will evoke a myriad of emotions…. However, you won't remain or sink in any one of the emotional moments because she expertly propels you into intentional searching and grabbing your internal power through very strategic, bottom-line sensitive exercises.

This Woman of God provides a lifeline, a foundation to help you identify internal and external resources which will enrich your life and help you embrace you, your purpose, and ultimate fulfillment of God's will for your life. Nekisha is academically credible which is good. The shared examples of her life story with all its pitfalls, pity parties, devastatingly wrong ill-advised decisions, insecurities, and her resulting understanding of her purpose to help others is so much greater. Your life will never be the same. As the late gospel artist extraordinaire Andrae Crouch sang…

I've had so many tears and sorrows; I've had questions for tomorrow; There's been many times I didn't know right from wrong. But in every situation; God gave me blessed consolation, that my trials come to only make me strong...Through it all I've learned to trust on Jesus, I've learned to trust in God...

Nekisha will not only give you the "how to's" but help you navigate through the ever-emerging emotions as you complete the questions and guidelines she's provided. She never leaves you as you travel through the mine fields of trashing every worry, nuisance, stressor as you discover the power within.

Christine Heath Diggs, Ph.D. MSSW, ACSW

Introduction

DYING TO BE A READY WOMAN

I will never forget the 21-hour drive from Houston Texas to Los Angeles CA. I packed everything I could in my Mercedes Benz S500, to include my then three-year-old daughter, in her car seat kicking her feet to the Donald Lawrence "Confessions" CD I had on loop. Here I was, appearing to be successful and having it all.

A master's degree possessing, internet radio personality with my own home-based Life Coaching business, married for 5 years and a mother. I was living in a beautiful townhome overlooking a lake where ducks and fish made their home, and for as impressive as it all seemed, MY truth had finally surfaced. All of these trappings were fillers for my empty soul, broken heart and belief that I was not worthy of happiness and I was not worthy of true love. So with hot tears running down my cheeks and my heart pounding with fear and anxiety I LEFT.

I finally got mad and tired enough to let it go and leave it all behind. That life looked good but was killing my soul, my personality and my ability to know what made me happy. I was married to an emotional wreck; a man whose character was likened to that of a cobra. He was the type whom everyone loved, and he'd give you the shirt off his back. He worked countless hours to ensure all of our bills were paid, and that we had everything we needed. However, I knew him as the ruthless, emotional abusive tyrant that made me feel like a helpless and hopeless little girl, in my own home. I was berated daily for not being good enough. I wasn't a good mother. I was too fat and too lazy. I was cursed at and ignored. He never wanted to go anywhere with me, nor did he invite me to his social gatherings, and he was always spoke in his native tongue.

One day, I got out of the house to attend a girlfriend gathering. My newly ex-husband, kept calling my cell phone, I didn't hear the ringing because it was in my purse. When I saw his missed calls, I tried to phone him back only to find that he'd had my cell phone service disconnected. He was punishing me for not being at his beck and call.

I remember countless arguments during which all he did was insult me by calling me stupid and an idiot. My mind flashes back to the time I was with our daughter at the park. She was about two years old and loved the sliding board. All of the kids were going up the sliding board and jumping from the top. I didn't realize my toddler was entertained by watching the other kids jump off. Before I knew it, she too had climbed to the top of the sliding board, and instead of sliding down, she jumped from the top. It was the big sliding board. So there I sat, watching my baby drop to the ground filled with dirt and woodchips.

She cried a little, but I was super nervous. I called my husband first to tell him what happened and he told me to meet him at home so we could take the baby to the hospital. Feeling sad and afraid I met him at home only to walk into an ambush of insults and belligerent behavior. He called me a stupid fat bitch, and accused me of allowing his baby to fall. Hollering that he was going to take his baby and get her a new mother, he snatched her from my arms and told me to shut up and get in the car. He cursed and fussed the entire ride to the hospital.

When we arrived at the emergency room, she was examined, and the doctor said she was fine and reassured my husband that this is a regular occurrence that children are curious and will do all kinds of things that put them in harm's way. My future ex-husband just looked at me with that evil smirk and remained quiet. Once he was sure the baby was okay, he took us home, then he went back out to work. There was no "I am sorry for overreacting", or any sign of remorse.

I'd like to say that, that was the only blowout, but there were so many that I had begun feeling remorseful for marrying this man. I should tell you, however, that it is my fault. I thought that because I was a plus-sized woman, I'd never have a chance at real love. He was the first man who had ever asked me to marry him as an adult, and I said yes. I didn't want to be alone. In fact, I hated being alone. I was the person who fantasized about being married and being a wife.

Five years was way too long to be in a relationship that wasn't feeding my soul, so after a 10-day juice fast, I decided there should be more to my life than being the target of his verbal and mental abuse. It hurt me to my core to leave him for the unknown, but I was dying inside.

I was more than a mother and homemaker; there was something inside of me that was sick and tired of feeling like I was the least of all; struggling and reliving the pain of being the target of another person's anger and hostility. Weary of being suppressed, inhibited and invisible; I was now ready to break the invisible chains of my life and emerge, unleash and answer the call ringing deep inside my soul to be free and happy on my terms. I was finally READY to live my life by my own rules and on my terms.

THE BOLD EXIT

I packed what I could while he was at work and got on the road to Los Angeles, CA. One thing I know for sure is when you're ready, you don't have to make an announcement, create an argument or evoke a dramatic exit. You just hold your head high, straighten your back, get what you need and boldly move into a new life. At least, that is what I did.

I wish I could say this was the only time RUNNING away from a situation was my solution. I had a habit of trying to please people who didn't love me and trying to take care of others while not taking care of myself. Not checking in on my feelings and what I wanted had become a habit. This time I had to deal with my barriers to my inner confidence and feeling like I never mattered. I decided to take a deep dive into the very essence of my soul, my core being and uncover all the trauma I tried to bury and forget. I may have looked like I was satisfied and happy, but that was not my truth; I was winging it. Trying to do things I thought would make me popular and well liked. Getting high from proving others wrong about what I could and could not do.

Deep down inside I never felt ready, and I never felt like I deserved any of what I had actually worked so hard for; it meant nothing and it wasn't fulfilling. I had this self-fulfilling prophecy that caused me to believe that as soon as I'd feel a little happiness it would be all taken away; akin to my foreclosed home, two car repossessions and a bankruptcy. Happiness was so very short-lived, and because I did not enjoy my life, I didn't like me or my life. The dislike showed up in everything, from lack of money to a lack of genuine love and relationships and the inability to feel like I could fit in.

The more I achieved, the more I lost. I could not build, I found myself rebuilding, restarting, redesigning but not evolving and stabilizing. In fact, one of my life-mentors, Debrena Jackson Gandy, asked me in her deep reflective and stimulating way, "Woman, why are you manifesting great things, and then breaking your magic wand?" I never had an answer.

I only knew that this was how it was for me. I would experience greatness and then it would be over, and I'd be back in the pit of just trying to make it.

When I realized my life was going in a ridiculous circle and I wasn't gaining anything; I stop trying. I became afraid to try because I knew eventually some disaster would come and take it all away. When big opportunities came to me, I would shrink and say, I am not ready. I needed to lose weight. I needed to have more education. I needed to have the right mentor. I needed more money.

I had an excuse for not leaping when the opportunity came. Later, I would find that someone else took the leap and I'd watch them live the life I wanted for myself. Mad as hell, I would feel rejected by God and life itself and become engulfed in a fury of envy. I was miserable as hell!

I still hadn't realized I hadn't dealt with the daemons in my past beginning with the emotional pitfalls I endured as a child, which bled into every area of my life, forcing me to repeat the same emotional shit.

I am not enough. Rejected, always second best, the strong gut-wrenching knots in the pit of my stomach reminded me I was too fat, too short, too loud, too needy, too fast, and too much of a risk. The feelings of fear and torment imparted to me by a well-meaning family that passed on to me, their anxieties and anger about life. Left in a long-time battle of my mind and spirit to entertain situations that reinforced my worthless feelings, I was spent.

I had mixed feelings about what I was good enough to have and who I was good enough for. Those mixed feelings ran my life, the life that I hated living. I was waiting for some miracle, or to be discovered, to be loved thoroughly, to be happy, to have prosperity, to create a movement that mattered, to ask for the sale, to get what I wanted. I was always waiting for the approval.

THE APPROVAL

I had not recognized that I was my own soul's enemy. I refused to follow my heart due to fear of letting others down which would then result in me being rejected and not being liked. I did not realize that the power to shape my world into the way I wanted to see it, had been and will always be inside of me.

I thought I needed permission to be okay with me. My thick thighs, my big butt, my big breast, my loud mouth, my big hair, my strong intuitive insight and entrepreneurial spirit, were ALL portions of me. I thought I needed permission to be me. In retrospect, I wasted time waiting for approval, for cheerleaders and the support and encouragement of others.

I finally found out that waiting for permission to be you and embrace the true you will eat away at your soul. Kill your soul purpose and the reason for being. I finally looked into the eyes of my soul and said what I had been waiting for so long to hear from others. I had been waiting for my parents to say and my family to realize and verbalize was that they were proud of me.

I could do anything, and no one could stop or hinder my purpose. The greatest revelation of all, was accepting that I am beautiful, lovable, intuitive, sensual and significant. I am BLISS! Where there is bliss, self-love exists.

When my soul feels good, it's all good. I didn't need permission; I just needed to break my invisible chains. I finally found out that I was the answer to my problems, unhappiness, and fears. I had to stop waiting for the world to endorse me and get in the driver's seat of my life, and start endorsing myself. I understand that many women struggle and fight with their greatness. Because we are trying to prove our worth to people who don't even know their worth, we end up losing sight of why we started the fight. Within eight months of arriving in Los Angeles, CA, I'd taken $1500 and created the life I'd always dreamed of.

My ex was shocked I had the balls to leave his mean ass, but he like many others could not believe I was doing it. I had two great jobs, a part-time business, my cute apartment and I was on the morning news segment of KTLA as a Relationship Expert. When you step into your READY WOMAN power, you are irresistible, unstoppable and influential.

Give yourself choices and opportunity to put the oxygen mask on you first before helping anyone else. That oxygen mask is love. Love is oxygen to the soul. If you don't love yourself, no one and I mean no one will love you either. You are the leader and CEO of your life. However, you can only lead when you are READY.

Of course, my ex did try everything to save this marriage, but when I decided to move, I moved on. I decided that I deserved more and I knew once I got myself and my life together, he would crave me and he did. I understood that for us to work, he needed to accept responsibility for his actions and do some work. He wasn't willing, and therefore, I filed for the divorce and received my freedom.

I learned how to be a Ready Woman, and that meant a woman of influence. Now prepare to read the private details, a diary so to speak, from my companions You should know that you are going through and went through that pain to get ready. I am going to teach you. It's a process of getting ugly and dirty first, but I promise by the end of reading this diary you will never lack anything when you embrace and unleash The Ready Woman inside of you.

THE READY WOMAN

The pages of this book are the paths and personal secret truths I experienced and very dark periods of my soul, tormented by situations in life that could have killed my desire to live out my unique purpose. Instead of giving up, I took responsibility for my life. I found resolve, acceptance and divine strength to rise up and unleash the superwoman power within.

This book is the recounting of situations that, although heart-wrenching, will leave you feeling speechless and determined to overcome the dark period of your life and turn that pain into a platform of influence and income. This book is the beginning to becoming a courageously authentic woman. A Ready Woman!

WHO IS A READY WOMAN?

A woman who will overcome her worse life challenge.

A woman who is fine with being vulnerable.

A woman who thrives to be a champion in every area of her life.

A woman who knows what she is made of greatness no matter what.

A woman who knows her experiences, her voice, her expertise and her pain MATTERS.

A woman who will break her invisible chains with the steps presented in this book.

ARE YOU READY to

1. Take charge of your soul and your story?

2. Turn each painful lesson into something beautiful and lasting?

3. Help others like you find their light and brilliance from the inside out?

A Ready Woman creates a new paradigm for her life with the belief that she is worthy of anything she wants. She can have love and live happily. All she must do is snatch her power back.

I learned how to be a Ready Woman, and that means a woman of influence, and now I am going to teach you. It's a process of going ugly and dirty first, but I promise by the end of this book you will never lack anything. It's your time to embrace and unleash The Ready Woman inside of you.

THE READY WOMAN MANTRA...

I now accept and receive; it takes Bliss, Grit & God to turn my challenges and problems into a platform for love, happiness, income & influence. Although I come as one, I stand as many because I am the Ready Woman.

THE OATH

I can, and I will live as a woman of income and influence because all the hell I've lived through was only to put me on the path toward The READY WOMAN. I accept the blessings and own the behavior and Bliss of the Ready Woman. I Am the Ready Woman today and always!

I am signing below for confirmation, That I Am the Ready Woman and accepts all lessons, rights, and blessings because of taking control of my soul and my life. As I read this book, I will incorporate the lessons immediately into my life so that I can experience my paradigm shift and welcome more happiness, love, income, and influence without doubt or disbelief.

Signature ____

Date ____

Chapter 1
Acknowledge the Nightmare

Soulfirmation:

"Before I ask for help, help is on the way;
the Universe is my friend and will support me in every way"

Bullied by Life

As a slave to my fears, I longed to be free. Every time I thought I was on my way to something better, I had only moved to what was, essentially, another slave plantation filled with bad experiences. Each of these bad experiences, which I did not know how to process or resolve, would soon cause me to start feeling as though I was being bullied by life.

My father, bless his heart, had no money and no stable place to call home. He had nothing tangible to offer. I can remember him showing me his paycheck stub, which revealed the meager amount of money he had left over after all the child support had been taken from all his baby mamas. Still, he managed to party and drink. I can remember him saying, "I can't wait until all y'all turn eighteen; then I can have something in my check. If I don't die first."

I remember how all his intimate relationships were with women who didn't mind taking care of him; he would not have it any other way. Whenever I got to spend time with Daddy, he would talk to me about his views and opinions. He said that white men can't be trusted because they stole from the Indians, and that everyone should have the courage to stand alone on their own two feet.

He also loved telling the story about how he was run out of Chattanooga, Tennessee, with nothing but the clothes on his back and the shoes on his feet.

Although my mother insisted that my dad was no good, I still felt a void on the inside. I wanted to spend more time with my father, but there was no telling how to get in touch with him because he moved around so much. As a matter of fact, it was a celebration when he would finally call or we would run into one of his friends who knew where to find him. I can now laugh at the many times I stayed up late, looking out the window, because he said he was on his way to come and get me.

But "on his way" could mean as many as two or three months from the time our conversation ended. When I got older, he would tell me that it wasn't his fault he was always missing-in-action. Either he didn't have transportation or my mom would piss him off and he didn't want to be bothered with her. But when he didn't show up, my mom would say, "See, I told you your father don't care about y'all."

Having no positive experiences with love, I became easy prey for early sexual exploitation by older cousins and teenage children of family friends. I didn't know it was wrong because it felt good after a while. Furthermore, I thought the more I gave, the more people would like me.

By thirteen, I was pregnant by a nineteen-year-old who exhibited many of my father's personality traits, and I immediately became a statistic. I felt like there were two labels stamped on my forehead: 'Inner City Youth at Risk' and 'Stupid Teenage Mother'. I was smart enough to know better because I was an honor-roll student. But in the words of my mother, "It's a shame to have book sense but no common sense."

When my mother talked to me about sex and behaving responsibly, she always spoke in a harsh, loud tone. "DON'T DO IT! And if you do it, and I find out you are doing it, I'll send you off to juvenile detention for girls." She used fear to try to control me, but it just was not enough to break the cycle of teen pregnancy - a cycle that had existed for generations in my family, although I didn't know it at the time because it was a big secret that no one talked about.

If you had asked me to explain life when I turned fourteen-years-old, I would have said that life is hell and I'm surrounded by bullies. The bullies of life picked on me because they knew that my foundation was rocky and emotionally out of control. I felt weak. No matter where I went or what I did, something chaotic and dramatic would always manifest, leaving me the center of confusion. It appears I had been branded with my bullies' initials to inform others that I was a slave. It was all right to be unappreciated and abused, and I could be treated as badly as anyone wanted to treat me. This was my reality.

I now understand that life was a struggle for my mother, and that could have been the major reason for her verbal and physical abuse. My schooling and career have helped me understand that you can't always judge and look down on how people choose to handle their problems. For my mother, and so many other struggling individuals in families, problems are not talked about; they are acted out. That can mean beating and cursing your spouse and kids, and drinking and drugging yourself sick. It's a way of coping, of demonstrating control or dominance, when in fact the feeling is powerlessness and emotional chaos.

An even clearer example of growing up in a household with an emotionally abusive mother is the 1981 film Mommy Dearest. The film is based on the life of actress Joan Crawford, told through the eyes of her adopted children. Joan was a mentally abusive wreck and no one could imagine that the most beautiful home on the block, and one of Hollywood's biggest stars, was filled with so much rage and that it was directed toward her innocent children.

In one scene, Mommy Dearest goes into the children's room while they're sleeping and admires the expensive things she could provide for them. She slowly fingers each precious item in Caroline's immaculate and orderly closet. Each blouse and dress is neatly attached to plastic or cloth hangers. She appears pleased, serene, satisfied... until she comes to a garment hung on a wire hanger. Then her serene expression dissolves into anger, and she screams, "Noooo wire hangers!" Caroline and her brother are ripped from deep sleep by their mother's ranting and raving. "What are wire hangers doing in your closet?" she demands, beating Caroline repeatedly and unmercifully with the wire hanger. "What are wire hangers doing in your closet?"

Growing up in my mother's home, I often experienced moments just like that. Much like Mommy Dearest, my mother associated love with giving things, but it didn't matter what she gave because of the dread I always felt when I was around her. I never knew when she was going to "go off" and get upset over something I didn't do to her satisfaction or liking

.

That dreadful feeling created a nest in my stomach and the nest would get bigger and bigger each time she screamed at me. She would curse and fuss and threaten me whenever she reached her boiling point. It didn't matter where we were—at home, at church, or wherever— she would go off and it was socially unacceptable for anyone within earshot to address it

.

Little did she know that every negative word she uttered, absent of nurturing and love, steadily fed the cesspool of resentment and self-hate that festered within me. They used to teach us, as children, to say "Sticks and stones may break my bones, but words will never hurt me." What a major fallacy that is. Words are what created my invisible chains.

As the oldest sibling, and only girl, I had the responsibility of co-parenting with my mother. In her defense, she was a young, twenty-something single parent of three children. Although she had a high school diploma, I believe she felt inadequate and thought that others viewed her the same way. She felt stuck and frustrated for never having enough and repeatedly looked-for work that would validate her skills and abilities. When she worked, it would often be long days or nights, making me responsible for my brothers.

In between her many jobs, I remember the welfare checks, the government cheese and butter, standing in the long lines to get the food stamps at the first of every month. I was the one who had to redeem them for groceries most of the time, hoping my friends wouldn't see me, even though most of them were living on food stamps too. In fact, almost everyone in my neighborhood received them.

I recall the time my mother had a meltdown because she lost her welfare check after having just cashed it at the grocery store. All the pressure, anger, and embarrassment she felt was directed toward me. I was just a little girl. What could I have done to correct this situation? Nothing, naturally, except take responsibility for it.

One thing I always did that brought me hope and inspiration was check out library books on African-American history, particularly about slavery. Harriet Tubman quickly became my favorite heroine. I was so intrigued by her because she'd grown up as a slave, but had the courage to run away.

More than that, she had the courage to return to the South to help other slaves escape. I would always say that I was going to escape my current situation because if Harriet could do it, then I could do it, too. I regularly daydreamed about escaping my night of hurt and pain. I made it my mission to find that place where I could feel free, where I could rid myself of feeling like I didn't belong.

Before I continue, let me just say that I know comparing my childhood to that of my ancestors who were slaves is extreme, but the daily routine I endured was itself a form of slavery. It was truly unbearable, and I was willing to do anything to escape it. Being awakened in the middle of the night and beaten because the dishes were not properly washed, something in the house was missing, or because my mother found out about something negative I'd said about her, was a normal occurrence. My mother had no emotional attachment to me, and she demonstrated that frequently through her violent outbursts.

When I was eleven years old, I had a big, thick Jheri curl. Anyone who has ever had a Jheri curl knows that after you wash the curl, it takes hours to activate and moisturize it so that it doesn't look like a dry, horrible Brillo Pad. In fact, it will lose its curl pattern, and your hair will just be sitting on top of your head, stiff and resistant and very hard to manage.

Being aware of all this, my mom decided to humiliate me by washing my hair right before Vacation Bible School. I was so angry and embarrassed, and I prayed that she would have a change of heart and not make me go with my hair looking like that. Besides, there was this cute boy named Jeremy in my class. As we approached the church, I said to my mother, "I am not going in there looking like this!" She grabbed my arm and forced me through the doorway. I saw all those people in the church and I yanked my arm from her. Before I knew it, my mom kicked my butt all over the church's front porch.

I believed that this would be the day that everyone would see how mean she was and someone would rescue me, but no one said a word. In fact, my grandfather took us back home where she continued what she had started. I wasn't allowed to use her bathroom, drink her water, or eat her food for the rest of the night.

Whenever I ran away, my grandparents always brought me back home, telling me that my mother didn't mean to do what she did to me and was sorry. I felt that I could never do enough to satisfy her. The more I did to try to please her, the more responsibility I was given, and the slightest mistake was a punishment in waiting— the phone cord or some other wire, her fist, and, almost every time, the most effective weapon of them all, her sharp tongue. My mother would often say how much she hated me, and I couldn't help but believe her. Eventually, I hated me, too. One time, Children's Services rescued me and my brother and sent us to live with my father.

The evidence against my mother was so bad that they arrested her for child endangerment. However, because I did not get along with my stepmother and my father wasn't as attentive to me as I had hoped, I recanted my story to my social worker after deciding that I'd much rather be living with my mother and sleeping in my own bed than be mistreated by my dad's wife. Besides, every time we went to court, I saw such pity and sadness in my mother's eyes.

I didn't want my mother to hurt, and I believed she was going to change and learn to control her temper just as she had promised. However, when the case was dropped and I went back to my mother's plantation, it didn't get better, it got worse. She didn't hit me as much, but her sharp tongue had become increasingly rough, and I learned to just live with it.

I didn't know of any defense mechanism to protect and uphold my value, my self-worth, or the positive self-image that I would rely on in order to succeed on so many levels in the years to come.

As a matter of fact, much of my life has been working to reverse the curse that has been unleashed on my life. My life is about breaking invisible chains, and this honest and revealing book will give you the courage and hope needed to break yours.

A Familiar Place

When I turned eighteen and graduated from high school, I escaped to college, from Ohio to Virginia, with a four-year-old little girl. I was determined to be free. While my family plotted against me, trying to convince me that I did not have what it took to raise a baby and go to school six hundred miles away from home, I was even more determined to prove them wrong. I had to prove them wrong because I was constantly being reminded of how I had messed up my life when I had a baby. How I had disgraced the family when I had the baby. How I couldn't do what others my age was doing because I had a baby.

Now that I was so far away, I thought that the bullies in my head that had directed my life in Ohio would disappear. What I soon realized was that bullies, like slave catchers, were on my trail; they had followed me to college. Even though I wasn't being hurt physically, I still felt the same dread, fear, and discontentment emotionally.

On many days, I felt like a tea kettle that's reached its full pressure from being heated on the stove and the steam can be seen blowing through the top. Whenever I felt this pressure it would make me cry and I didn't always understand why I was crying. All I knew was that something on the inside was suffocating me and limiting where I went and who I talked to. It made me afraid of my environment and afraid to tell the truth. Additionally, I worried more about not hurting others than I cared about making myself happy. I sacrificed to gain the respect of my peers and found out that it didn't matter because the deep-rooted self-hatred in my mind said to me, "You are never going to be good enough."

I eventually started thinking about a way to kill myself. I pondered driving my car into a tree with my daughter inside. I didn't want to leave her behind and risk the possibility of one of my family members raising her because her life might turn out the way mine did. If I was leaving, she was going with me.

Ultimately, I had grown too afraid to take my own life. I wasn't too godly at the time, but somehow, I believed that there was a heaven and a hell. I feared that I would go to hell if I killed myself. Although I didn't really want to live and life had become hopeless for me, ending my life seemed too complicated and scary. So, there I was—stuck. And how did it show? Multiple sex partners, an inability to have stable relationships, loud, obnoxious language, trying to be the center of attention, criticizing others, and feeling envious toward my friends who seemed to have the perfect life.

The Boogie Man is Real

One morning, I woke up after a big fight with the man I thought was my soul mate to find out he was gone. All his belongings, half of the furniture, the stereo, the microwave it was all gone. My low income 2-bedroom apartment in the center of Petersburg, VA was dark, quiet and now half empty. You see, Rob and I met when I was 15 years old and a freshman in high school. He was a grade ahead of me and although initially he didn't like me because of my loud, very vocal and opinionated personality, something happened when he finally asked me for my phone number. We became inseparable.

We talked for hours on the phone, sharing the most secretive and intimate details of our lives. After about a year of just talking and smiling at each other, our relationship progressed into romance. We were like brother and sister, we were best friends and we were lovers. We did everything together and it felt so good that finally something in my life wasn't a struggle. For the first five years of our relationship, we were as close as close could be until I delayed our marriage and chose college instead. Rob followed me to school and he worked while I went to school.

Then the jealous rages started, he began hitting me, yelling at me, and smoking marijuana. He worked less and left me responsible for making sure everything was taken care of in the house. Our relationship became overwhelming and hard.

We had arguments before but this time he beat me with the phone and I knew that it would probably get worse. I decided to stand up for myself and show him that his behavior wasn't okay. So, I told him to leave but my intention was for him to leave long enough to cool down and realize his behavior was out of control. I didn't mean for him to leave me in Petersburg, in a dark, cold empty apartment all by myself. I didn't mean for him to relocate all the way back to Ohio.

I didn't mean for him to find a new woman and start a family with her. I didn't mean for him to ignore my calls, beg me to leave him alone and distance himself from me. I didn't mean for him to take his family away from me. Five years of my life, I grew up with Rob and everyone thought we were the couple to envy and we were in so many ways.

The Boogie Man is so real in that in the one area of my life I thought I was mastering it turned out to be the beginning of many more nightmares.

I had two very best friends in high school. Phillip and Ursula. Phillip became my best friend during computer science. I had no idea what was going on in that class and he always rescued me, partly because I kept him laughing when he was my partner and partly because he may have had a slight crush on me. I don't know for sure because he won't admit it. However, I remember being so hungry and so broke and Phillip would always have money.

When I realized how giving he was, without expecting anything in return, our friendship really grew. It almost grew past friends to brother and sister. In fact, his parents were my parents and there were so many times I prayed and wished I could be their daughter. They were my best examples of "The Cosby Show" family. I enjoyed being around him and just having fun. We did everything together in and out of school.

My friend Ursula's family treated me just like Phil's, although Ursula was from a single parent home. I liked Ursula because she was nowhere near five feet tall, but had a mouth as if she was six feet tall. I liked Ursula because she was so giving and forgiving. Her mother was the same height as her but they both had such big hearts. They valued each other and family meant so much to them.

I didn't feel lost when I was around Phillip and Ursula. I thought that after graduation we would all go to college together, but we all went our separate ways. However, our freshman year we talked on the phone all the time and planned how we would spend our summer vacation when we returned home so that we could be united and reminisce about the old times. However, during the summer between our freshman and sophomore year in college, life just became too intense and the fun stopped for a long time.

Both of their siblings were killed tragically a month apart. Phillip's sister, Niaya, was killed in a horrible automobile accident. She was on her break from work and went to run an errand. Her car was struck on the highway by another motorist and exploded. Niaya died instantly. The motorist who caused the accident was never found.

Phillip was supposed to pick me up from the airport since I was the last to arrive home from college. He called me at my apartment as I prepared for my departure; I thought to make sure I was getting on the plane. I will never forget that. I thought it was a

joke because none of my peers had ever experienced something so tragic. I was so spooked and traumatized by the accident that I began to avoid situations that I felt I had no control over. I stayed at Phillip's parents' house and got the food ready for the guests after the funeral because I knew it would prevent me from attending the service.

I did not want to see his sister and be reminded of death or dying. Prior to this, I had always believed that bad things happened to bad people. However, for something like this to happen to a good person like Niaya, I knew my turn was around the corner because of all the bad I had done. It was also around this time I started having anxiety attacks but was not aware of what they were.

A month later, Ursula and I were planning to go job searching. I remember her calling me and saying that as soon as she got dressed, she would come and get me. If Phillip hadn't already found a job, all three of us would be going. That's how close we all were.

Forty-five minutes after I hung up with Ursula, she called me back, screaming and hollering. Somebody had done a drive-by on their house and shot her brother, Terry. He had been sitting in front of the television eating breakfast. He was rushed to the hospital, but didn't make it.

He died later that evening. The drive-by was meant for the people in the house next door who were associated with drugs. Terry was innocent. He was a working college student attending the Ohio State University. He too was a good person who died too young. This further reinforced my belief something bad was going to happen to me next.

I had no other choice but to attend Terry's funeral. I cried, kicked, and screamed, but Ursula refused to let me stay home. She fussed at me until I agreed to go to the service with my mother. However, I sat so far in the back by the exit that I didn't even know what the casket looked like or what was being said. I was too afraid to see or hear anything and I mentally blocked out everything so I wouldn't be affected by my surroundings.

I was being haunted by yet another Boogie Man - physical death. Old folks used to say that death travels in threes, so I knew one of my siblings—if not me— had to be next. They are both still fine, thank God, but the fear of death had me emotionally crippled for many years, until I was forced to deal with the passing of my grandmother, Mama Maggie.

I now understand that anything you are afraid of will keep confronting you until you deal with it. The negative forces in my head eventually became stronger and stronger because a war had eventually broken out in my thoughts between life and death, and truth and untruth. Furthermore,

I did not know how to process it all. Most of all, I had no one in my life who cared enough about me to take my hand and tell me it was going to be all right. I felt like I was losing control and I started feeling a tightness in my chest.

My breathing became shallow, pain filled my arms, and I had recurring stomachaches. My mind and body felt weak and I felt like I was floating on air. Nothing seemed real. It scared me so much.

Ambulances transported me to emergency rooms when I felt pains in my chest that I thought were heart attacks. Within hours, I would be released from the hospital with a prescription to treat acid reflux. My medical chart thickened. I knew there was something more to what I was feeling than met the eye. It was so hard to explain to the medical professionals.

My physical ailments were always accompanied by that dreadful feeling that I had become so accustomed to. It took some time, but the emergency room advised me to follow up with a family doctor, and I did. After all, I was extremely good at being accommodating.

During an examination for a routine check-up, my primary care physician asked me a series of questions pertaining to my physical symptoms. I was relieved that someone finally understood what was going on with my body and wasn't blaming it on acid reflux.

Just when I was getting excited about him describing the symptoms and nodding my head in agreement, he dropped the bomb and gave me my diagnosis. His explanation went like this:

"Nothing is wrong with your blood pressure, your heart, or your lungs. Your kidneys and bladder are fine, and your bloodwork is fine. The problem is that something or someone broke your heart and your mind is playing tricks on you. You are depressed. Not only are you depressed, but you're experiencing episodes of anxiety. These things are a result of previous trauma that has not been dealt with appropriately. I want you to make an appointment with a therapist and follow the directions on the medication I will prescribe for you. With the two – the medication and the therapy – you will be fine."

My mind was playing tricks on me? Depression? Anxiety? This couldn't be true. I associated mental illness with other people who just couldn't handle life. My ego started defending my claim. I was handling my life. I was a freshman in college, working on my bachelor's in social work. I was on the dean's list and holding a part-time job while raising my little girl alone. Last, but not least, I was well on my way to proving to myself that I could be a better mother than my own mother had been and that I could handle school and being a parent at the same time.

And now the doctor was telling me that I needed professional help because I was mental?! After my visit with the doctor, I refused to tell anyone about what was going on within me. How could I? On the outside, people see my bubbly personality; however, now I was worried that no one would take me seriously and I would be exposed to be nothing more than a broken pitiful person. The Boogie Man in my head would say,

"See, you ain't gonna be nothin', just like your mother said!"

I couldn't share this with my mother because she would somehow convince me that she had tried to tell me I had a problem and was a problem my whole life and somehow would convince me to come home so she could continue to control my life. And due to some extreme behaviors, I saw exhibited in the church growing up, I was not a big fan of religion and didn't seek God, although I believed in Him.

However, a year later, I was getting worse even though I was taking my pills and going to therapy. It was temporary relief, and I had nowhere else to run to. I felt trapped and burdened under the weight of something that I had no control over. I was intertwined in it and I did not have a clue as to how to get free from it. One dark night, I felt a pulling in my gut, which led me to dust off the Bible I had received as a graduation present from my former church. For several nights in a row, I read aloud the only passage of scripture I knew:

"The Lord is my shepherd, I shall not be in want. He makes me lie down in green pastures, He leads me beside quiet waters, He restores my soul He guides me in paths of righteousness for His name's sake. Even though I walk through the valley of the shadow of death, I will fear no evil, for you are with me; your rod and your staff, they comfort me. You prepare a table before me in the presence of my enemies. You anoint my head with oil; my cup overflows. Surely goodness and love will follow me all the days of my life, and I will dwell in the house of the Lord forever."

– Psalm 23, NIV.

The Silent Cry for Help

I was growing more tired of feeling sad and being bullied than ever before, and somehow, I knew that if I was going to find any hope of freeing myself, for once in my life, I needed to be confident. I needed to know I wasn't alone and that the answer or help I needed was already here; I just needed to acknowledge its presence.

There comes a time when there are no more tears left to cry and nothing else is working out. Even if you never prayed a single prayer before, something in your soul knows that the answer is God and that He is real. Something in my soul knew that it was going to take God's power to fix what pills and doctors alone could not.

I learned in my darkest night that you learn what you're made of and sometimes it takes courage to live through another moment. Not another hour or day, but another moment. I silently asked for help sitting all alone in my room. Surprisingly, help was already here. What I am going to show you through my life, is that just because you have a nightmare doesn't mean that you stop dreaming.

Step 1: Acknowledge the Nightmare

Journal Soul Work:

1. When you call for help what do you expect to happen?
2. What does it take for you to ask for help?
3. What is your Boogie Man?
4. What nightmare do you need to acknowledge and how will you tell your story?
5. With whom will you share your nightmare and what do you expect to happen?

Chapter 1 Expansion Exercise: "Reacting vs. Responding"

The reason most self-help gurus share their personal story is to help those reading or listening to it resonate and identify key aspects of learning through the subject matter. In chapter one, "Acknowledge the Nightmare", I reveal my earliest recollection of feeling emotionally out of control, bullied and rejected.

What parts of my story resonate with you and why?

____

____

____

____

____

What insights do you have about your past that help you understand your current situation with love and relationships?

____

____

____

____

____

In what way did you feel bullied by your life?

____

____

____

____

____

When feelings of rejection, abandonment, being bullied and disappointed by life surface, does it remind you of past circumstances you have had to overcome or live through?

____

____

____

____

____

What is your normal reaction to these unpleasant feelings?

____

____

____

____

____

Reacting is a negative pessimistic coping mechanism that causes you to allow fear to dictate your actions. Reacting is a lower vibration and creates harsh, sad and hostile consequences both internally and externally.

Responding is a positive optimistic way of permanently resolving unpleasant circumstances using a love based modality and a healthy pattern of thought. Responding is a higher vibration frequency and attracts to it long term peace, growth and well-being.

In Chapter 1, I shared with you my reaction when I encountered unpleasant feelings was to run away, also known as flight or fight. Once I realized that my emotional state could not be handled by running away or by medication, I stopped reacting and learned to respond. Psalm 23 from the Holy Bible became my primary soul-firmation, which is my positive affirmation, to build my faith that I am supported by unseen forces that have my best interest in mind. I started responding by doing deep soul searching into the root cause of my feelings and seeking a deeper understanding of the best way to gain control of my soul by reaching out for supernatural help.

Now that you know the difference in reacting vs. responding, let's explore where you can begin to do more responding vs. reacting to knee jerking unpleasant situations and circumstances.

For example, if you feel rejected and you normally get angry and become dismissive, a good place to start could be getting quiet in your mind and repeat to yourself that you are cared for and a better opportunity is very near. In essence you are reframing the situation and giving it a new meaning that is lighter and more positive.

Personal Response Plan

Reacting		Responding	
How do you feel in unpleasant situations and circumstances	How do you react to this feeling?	What is the opposite of this feeling?	How can you let go of this feeling and respond with love?
Example: Rejected	Example: Angry and dismissive	Example: Cared for	Example: Quiet my mind and repeat, "I am cared for and a better opportunity is near."

Chapter 2

Align Your Soul

Soulfirmation::

My soul moves from mourning the nightmare to morning joy as I actively decide to evolve out of my pain and fears.

A Cry for Help

While living with my private pain and secret of being a mental case, I was depressed but functional. I was moving forward with my degree program in social work and I served as an intern during my senior year in college. This put me in direct contact with adolescents who were at high risk of dropping out of school.

One day I was conducting a group session with the students. One of the participants, an African-American boy, began making negative comments and being disruptive during a group session. He was determined to be oppositional, confrontational, and very disruptive. I had never witnessed such obscene behavior displayed by him or any of the other youths before, and I saw an opportunity to exert my control as the authority figure. Since I was depressed, control was something I yearned to exhibit. Being the authority figure in this situation felt so good.

Had I been intuitively aligned, I would have heard his soul crying. I would have recognized the pain he was feeling was identical to my own pain. Instead, I allowed my emotions of superiority get the best of me. He was in mental and emotional pain. He probably lacked the vocabulary to share what he was feeling and didn't think anyone would care. He acted out his aggravation and agitation through negative behavior just like we do with our mates and those closest to us. Instead of sharing what's hurting we act out in extreme ways as to push the person away. We do the opposite of what we really desire, which leaves us with a self-fulfilling prophesy that no one cares and that we are alone.

I remember this day like it was yesterday. I sternly looked this young man in the eye and told him that he had a couple of options: Stop the negative behavior and participate in the group appropriately or get to steppin' and leave the group altogether. Much to my surprise, the young man chose the second option and left the group abruptly.

At the time, I firmly believed that I had made the right decision. I felt that prohibiting that one student from disrupting the flow of activities would get me the respect I wanted from the rest of the class and allow me to maintain the control I so desperately needed as a young intern. Following my ego and not my soul cost me something that night. Reacting instead of responding left a permanently etched consequence that diminished my self-esteem and belief in my ability to be a confident and capable social worker.

That same night I had a visit from the familiar dread that used to nest in the pit of my stomach and would overtake me when I knew my mother was upset with me and when I obsessed over ending my life. It was nauseating and intense. Once again, I felt a strong urge to die. This had always been my first response to threatening situations that appeared as though there was no other way out. I really felt as though my life had no real purpose, I was confused, so unhappy and just feeling like a complete failure.

I gasped for air. I was having a panic attack. I was trying hard to focus my mind in another direction, but the feeling was too strong. I had to call for help and I had to do it quickly. Something was about to happen and I was truly afraid. I really believed that I was about to die. Actually, something worse did happen and I felt it. I got the courage to call a minister at my church and before I could explain anything to him he just started to pray for me. The prayer calmed my nerves and a peaceful presence entered the dark space in my soul.

That night, a suicidal presence tried to overtake my soul. I struggled with it because my soul was uneasy and my conscious was not at peace. My soul was not in alignment and that created a war in my mind and emotions. I didn't know how to soothe my pain. Despite what my mother had always said to me, I did have some common sense because I was sensible enough to phone someone I knew who had a significant relationship with the Divine that was powerful enough for me to believe in.

I learned that night that when the soul cries, it really doesn't want to die; it wants to be nourished, it wants to be listened to, fed, and it wants some TLC. My decision to rescue my crying soul and see another day made all the difference through the power of prayer and intercession from another. The minister who prayed for me was intuitive and understanding that I was emotionally unstable, fearful and hurting and he knew exactly what to do.

Unfortunately, I didn't realize that someone else's soul was crying. There was danger on another plantation of fear, hurt and disappointment; another emotional slave was being bullied by life, and suicide was his method of escape. I need you to brace yourself for what I am about to reveal... As I returned to my internship the next day, my students rushed into the classroom to tell me some horrific news.

The disruptive student that I had made leave the group the previous day, the young man that I had told to get to steppin', had stepped out of this life by shooting himself in the head. He had been added to the statistic which states that the third leading cause of death for young people between the ages of fifteen and twenty-five is suicide. I suffered another blow to my confidence and belief in me. I was not able to discern the same issues in him that I was facing. I had manifested a kid in my life that was also facing the same soul conflict but he didn't have the support I did and he did not know how to sooth his crying soul.

It dawned on me that the Boogie Man has the most power over those of us who are looking for the fastest way to escape the hurt and pain. He preys on those of us who do not know what to do when our souls begin to cry. It was unnerving to think that at sixteen years old, my student had made the final decision to escape the Boogie Man in his life by such brutal means.

He must have found it really hard to allow his soul to go on aching with pain and shame. Can you imagine the intense regret and remorse I felt upon learning that this student had given in to the ultimate self-destruction? I realized that, just like me, he didn't know how to feed his soul and the invisible chains in his life were driving him insane

My emotions were paralyzed. I was afraid and mad at God. Somehow, more than ever, I felt that I had a personal commitment to help my fellow emotional slaves to invisible chains find the Promised Land without using the suicide route.

Even though it was a constant struggle for me, the death of my student gave me a deeper reason to keep my hope of finding freedom alive. I had an epiphany then; I was going to be the Moses of emotional healing, the way that Harriet Tubman was the Moses of the Underground Railroad for black slaves in America.

One way or another, I would figure out how to get free, and then I would spread the word to others the method to set them free. I began to believe more than ever that my purpose was wrapped up in my secret. In my heart, I knew it was time for me to get free or die trying.

I felt like I had helped life bully my student right to his grave. With the time I had, I could have remembered the fact that he had never acted out in my class before.

I could have taken him aside and given him unconditional acceptance and kind words. However, I wanted to be in control and squash his 'bad' behavior and my fear of 'losing' to some kid was my motivation for a quick fix.

I know what he did was not my fault, but just think that if I had taken a little time to find out what was going on with him, I would have realized that he was feeling rejected and disappointed by his girlfriend, his other teachers, and his parents.

I now understood that I could not give him what I did not have to give. Invisible chains don't give you the freedom to move outside of what has always been familiar. I was okay acting out what I had lived even though I despised it.

That incident reinforced that I was the enemy that I hated. I consistently recreated situations that kept me locked up with the same emotions of pain, fear and trepidation that I grew up with.

I kept reliving situations that put me in a place where I continued to struggle and be abused. This was normal to me, this was all I knew. I didn't recognize that my soul was crying because I didn't know that there was anything more to life than pain, disappointment, fear and struggle.

Why Suicide?

In my quest to understand the route to freedom I learned to pray. I was looking for answers because I felt that life was so unfair. I started going to church more frequently. I kept getting that urge in my stomach to spend more private time reading my Bible and finding books on how to pray. As I became more comfortable with praying, I started to hear a small voice that seemed to be coming from my stomach talk to me about questions I had been asking God to answer.

I believe that suicide becomes attractive to the crying soul. Suicide can look so many ways but ultimately it is simply a way to give up on your life. People give up on life with drugs, alcohol, and risky lifestyles that include danger and self-harm.

Suicide is when you feel powerless over the demons of your life and you surrender to them by way of self-destruction. It can include child abuse, murder, repeat criminal activities, abusive relationships and chronic food addiction.

The crying soul is your mind, will, and emotions feeling trapped in a losing battle of disappointment. The crying soul is losing its tolerance to endure, it is becoming numb, it is becoming blind to purpose and completely disappointed with the little understanding it has of God. Confused about life and its meaning, the crying soul sees that there is nothing but a void that cannot be filled.

The crying soul is either ignoring the opportunity to commune with God or it does not understand how to commune with God and is obsessed with dwelling on all that is wrong. The strongest memories and energy are derived from all the perceived wrong that you have experienced and/or witnessed.

At this point, the will is weak and there is no fortitude to see what the future has to offer. The soul finds comfort by contemplating and plotting an end. It wants to move on to a better place where there will be no more hurt or pain.

The voice of the Boogie Man becomes louder and louder in your head and is overwhelming. You honestly believe that life would be better without you and even God is powerless to change your situation.

There is a squeeze on the inside that feels like it will never go away. The only way for you to gain control, according to the voice of the Boogie Man, is by ending it all. The revelation I got about the squeeze is that this is a time in life when we are walking through the valley of the shadow of death, as stated in the 23rd Psalm. Many don't understand, as I do now, that we will all walk through the valley of the shadow of death and it feels like death. It is actually the ego fighting to stay in control of your thinking and being.

The ego is resistant to you finding your Divine strength and abilities to explore change and transformation. So in between where you are and where you really want to be is the battle of your life. It is the battle of change and having the confidence to know that the universe completely supports you changing to obtain your higher most powerful good.

It is said that the ego will fight against anything that is different than what it's used to. The ego doesn't want to be annihilated and in metaphysics this is the metaphorical devil that ruins our lives and fights us when we decide that enough is enough.

The Universe Supports Us

The answer to being able to overcome or walk through the squeeze, according to Psalm 23, is understanding that the universe supports us regardless of how we feel, and it can even turn the worst situation around and cover us with a beautiful Divine presence and light. The challenge, of course, is to understand, learn and be patient enough to invite the Divine presence into our lives and be in a place to listen and adhere to the instruction given. This instruction is called inspired action because you are in the spirit. It's the inward prompts to do the opposite of what you are currently doing that's getting you nowhere but in a sad pattern of hopelessness.

The first few lines of the 23rd Psalm reveal how God leads us to all the good, peaceful, and prosperous places. The next section addresses how we get off course in life or are walking away from God.

I found that God's presence and warmth leads us back to the place where the soul can rest and be restored. We will find comfort in our communion with God when we trust that the universe will deliver to us all that we need and hope for. Healing is about trusting and patience. The more patience we have and the more we trust, the more we will feel different.

Healing Emotional Wounds

Physical wounds result from bumps, bruises and scrapes. Some are more severe than others.

There are medicines and ointments that speed up the healing process when these injuries occur. Oftentimes, we heal so well that our physical scars are unnoticeable. What about the healing of emotional wounds? What can we use to help heal them? The medicine I recommend is spirituality and a stable, consistent interaction with God.

That is the only medicine tough enough to completely heal the crying soul. Your ability to invite God into your life changes everything, and we will discuss this in a later chapter.

Invisible chains are created when emotional wounds are not healed and they stifle you. Every painful memory that you carry within your soul is a link that creates the chain. They are generations of cursed words and private pain. If these links are not broken, the invisible chains will forever keep you a slave to all issues that damage your ability to honor your spirit, your soul, your body and ultimately the Divine presence within you.

Your negative perception of your past keeps you stifled, frustrated and most often broken in spirit and in your wallet. Living with invisible chains forfeits your right to happiness and bliss. However, the power of the invisible chains is a part of your subconscious programming. Subconscious programming drives your behaviors and attracts majority of your life experiences. The subconscious mind controls your feelings until you become conscious of your patterns and programming.

Breaking the Silence

For a period of time, I relied on anti-depressants to fix me and give me a small dose of happiness. I would literally watch the clock, anxiously awaiting the next dose, because the previous dose had lost its effect and I disliked the feeling of reality. The medicine, for the most part, dulled the feeling of anxiety that had settled in the pit of my stomach years earlier. It helped me get through the days without feeling out of control and sad.

Dealing with my strong negative emotions and pain was very challenging because my spirituality was underdeveloped. It was like stepping into a new world I knew absolutely nothing about.

I understood church but I did not understand how to create a spiritual connection so that I would not feel that I didn't belong on earth. Besides that, I couldn't always pinpoint why I was feeling the way I did day in and day out. All I knew was that something had a hold on me and I couldn't see what it was. I could feel it and it would not let me go.

I promised God that if I was helped, I would not be ashamed or embarrassed to profess, acknowledge and give Him honor when He delivered me.

I told Him I would help anyone He wanted me to help and I would not hold in my secret any longer. I would let people know that there are monsters, devils, and Boogie Men who will destroy the gift of life. I want you to know God heard me and I was answered. God hears you too and is answering you now.

It's Time

When the soul cries, we must remember it is a sign that it is impossible to live without the presence of God and for many that could mean being grounded and connected to yourself and to your divinity. Healing cannot happen if you are not connected inwardly to your main source of power supply. Many of us neither understand nor have ever experienced God's presence.

This is mostly because our parents were so preoccupied with material things and taking care of basic needs that they forgot or did not know how to teach us to do things that will allow our spirits to thrive. Even if they went to church, the mosque, temple, etc. and we went along with them, we saw it as just a weekly regimen.

We weren't really taught to put God first, so we didn't even know what that consisted of. Because of the practice of religion and the lack of spirituality, we didn't have a clue about what to do when our souls began to cry out in pain and emptiness.

Many of us missed the part of growing up where we got to learn our heritage, what we're made of and how to discover who we are. We were taught to go to school, be good and make a good life for yourself but how do you make a good life for yourself when you've experienced so much turmoil, pain and confusion in the early years?

The answer to healing from injury is time. It takes time to build a relationship with God and it takes time to build a relationship with the authentic self. However, it is God's presence that dwells within us to free us from all the chains to get us into our perpetual state of bliss. God will give us the power to be free and the yearning to listen to the voice of God, which will guide and lead our inspired actions. Pain allows us the opportunity to explore how powerful we are to redirect our lives to a place that's forgiving, compassionate and leads to wholeness.

It allows us to realize that we shouldn't take anything for granted and although life can hurt, the ultimate design is to make us more powerful beings with the authority to co-create lives that are happy, abundant and loving. The healing power of the Divine helps us to understand that we are cared for even when it feels as if no one else cares for us. Pain is invisible, so it takes the invisible to overcome it. It takes a supernatural remedy to bring peace and comfort to a troubled soul.

The challenge for those of us who are used to running away, like I was, is that we run away from everything and we don't give anything or anyone the opportunity to help us, including God. We are sometimes too frightened and confused, making spirituality harder than it really is. We easily believe all the untruths and illusions instead of believing what is true and real. Therefore, looking to God as a remedy to heal and help us break the invisible chains seems unrealistic. As physical beings, we should see something in order to believe it. How many times have you heard the phrase "seeing is believing?"

The mind is powerful. It sees what it wants to believe. For example, doctors have used placebos in tests for years. A placebo is a pill that contains no medication. It is often used in clinical studies to assess the effectiveness of the real drug. Patients do not know if they receive the drug or placebo and sometimes the patients who receive the placebo report that they no longer have the symptoms which required the drug.

In other words, a doctor can give you a fake pill and tell you that it will relieve your headache. If you swallow the placebo and believe it will cure your headache, you may think that the headache is gone. Why? Because you took a pill and believed it had the power to stop your pain

The ego uses placebos to keep us in our old programming. The placebo is all of the destructive behaviors and people that we use to ignore the pain that we have within us. We don't understand how to use the power of our minds for healing and manifestation or we are unwilling to connect with God. It feels like it is so much easier to try to ease the pain with the placebo during tough times, thinking that it is what we need to make us feel better. We want it quick, therefore, we tend to disregard God and use people and things as a substitution: therapists, psychics, sex, overeating, alcohol, and drugs.

These things become our gods because they feel good to the body and soul and trick us into believing that we are escaping our problems. However, they keep us chained with a crying soul. That is how the Boogie Man succeeds in keeping us running and burying our problems. This becomes a self-destructive life pattern. We will continue to be emotional slaves if we keep handling our problems and things the same way instead of looking to God and allowing the power to provide us with inner power and direction to bring us to the Promised Land of serenity.

The lesson here is that you must confront the root of your programming, not treat the symptoms that you display when trying to hide by using placebos. Treating the symptom quiets the pain temporarily, but treating the root causes real internal positive change. In order to go through change that will last you must have the spiritual maturity to acknowledge that you need something more than material things can offer.

You need the super and the natural working together. You need to experience things that are too hard to explain to others. You need God and God wants a relationship with you. When is the last time you checked in with God, the super, to allow him to reveal what you can do in the natural? There are questions I want you to ask yourself every time you feel out of control or you feel like life just isn't fair

1. Are you feeling connected to the Divine?
2. What have you been thinking about and worrying over?
3. Who are you protecting, how are you protecting them and why?
4. Why are you here?
5. What is your regimen to realign yourself with the Divine?

Whether you like it or not, whether you believe it or not, the answer is within YOU! Shh! Listen! Is your soul crying? It is up to you to give it what it really needs.

Step 2: Align Your Soul

Chapter 2 Expansion Exercise: "Responding to the Soul Cry"

The more understanding we have of ourselves, the better we are able to respond versus react to the cues, prompts, or warnings that we sense emotionally. Therefore, there is a misalignment in our souls that cause fragmented relationships especially when it comes to love and romance. My soul cry was heard through anxiety attacks and suicidal ideation. Instead of taking my life, I began asking deeper questions, like "Why is suicide so attractive?" Why is the initial reaction to the soul cry to destroy my life?

It's time to break your silent suffering. It's time to break free of the issues, events and experiences that make you want to disappear forever. Problems may make you want to disappear, call it quits or do something erratic each time you feel hurt, overwhelmed or engulfed in pain. This is the platform and the time to allow it to flow out.

When you tell your story, you free the pressure that's boiling within. You tell your story to feel better and you tell your story until it no longer hurts. The issue is often we tell our story in fragments but not in totality. It's time to get it all out, tell your story and be free of the shame, embarrassment, confusion and pain. Tell it until you can laugh about it.

1. Find a medium to tell your whole story and keep telling it over and over until its power does not control you. Examples are:

- Record a video
- Write a book
- Journaling
- Audio recording
- Public Speaking
- Write yourself a letter
- Poetry
- Song
- Artwork

2. Be conscious of each time you are reminded or triggered of a past life hurtful event. What do you do? How do you react? What do you reach for? How do you feel?

Be conscious of your reaction patterns. Use the Personal Response Plan provided in the Chapter 1 Worksheet to track these reactions.

3. Now let's take your Personal Response Plan one step further... Take your reactions and communicate with the Divine. Ask yourself why is this your perception of the event? Why is that your reaction? What are the consequences or outcomes from your reaction? Who wins? Who loses? What do you gain from this reaction? What do you lose when you react like this?

Reaction	Why is this my perception?	Why do I react in this manner?	What are my consequences / outcomes if I react like this?	Who wins and who loses with this reaction?	What do I gain?	What do I lose?

.

.4. Name some instances when your soul cried and what did it feel like? What did your soul need? Did you give it what it needed or what it was crying for?

____

____

____

____

Now that you know that your soul cries and when it cries it's a sign that it needs some nourishment from the Divine and TLC from you, it is important to refer to your Personal Response Plan created in the Chapter 1 Worksheet. Your plan helps you ensure that your soul is soothed in the right way. Responding instead of reacting is the optimistic and healthy way of providing self-love and optimum self-care.

Below are examples of how you can nourish your soul when it cries:

- Taking a hike
- Sitting at the beach
- Attending a spiritual service
- Talking to a coach/therapist
- Journaling
- Praying
- Fasting/Cleansing
- Joining a support group
- Playing with childre
- Pampering myself
- Visiting a great restaurant
- Painting
- Taking a vacation
- Taking a spiritual retreat
- Reading
- Affirming my worth and value
- Exercising
- Listening / Watching Inspirational Programming
- The list goes on...

Continue adding to this list periodically and watch your programing shift to peace and harmony and your pain shift to abundant joy. It's the little things that make the greatest impact

.

5. Every time you are conscious of your shift from reacting to responding you deserve to be celebrated. What will you do to celebrate your success?

____

____

____

____

____

Chapter 3
Reboot Your Spirit

Soulfirmation:

As my soul bonds with Good, I am better able
to understand myself and create a life that feels good.

Your spirit is not the same as your soul. Typically, the words for soul and spirit are used interchangeably, however, they are not the same. Your soul makes up your identity. It is how you feel, how you think, what you believe and what you do. Everything is bundled as one, which shares the same residence as what we refer to as the living soul. Your spirit on the other hand is your divinity.

It is where your supernatural power lives and it is where you gain insight, which comes directly from the universe and your higher power. The spirit is that part of you that when you are fully connected to your divinity, drives your soul to ultimate optimisms and gives you the inspiration (in spirit) to overcome challenges, expand your conscious awareness and attract goodness and unmerited blessings into your existence.

It is your spirit that is the powerhouse of healing, well-being, intuition, and conversations with the Divine. Your connected spirit makes your aura bright, your appearance attractive and fuels your confidence. You may have heard the reference before, "he or she has a broken spirit." What it really means is she is feeling disconnected from the divine.

When we talk about not having confidence, what we're really saying is that there is a disconnection from the divine. The reason I believe as I do, is because during the many years that I struggled with my self-esteem and confidence, the times that I struggled with purpose and feeling as if I belonged, it all traces back to how I was feeling about my connection to God. When I felt my worse, I felt the furthest away from God. I felt that God was punishing me and that I was forgotten.

In working with hundreds of clients who also experienced a lack of self confidence, once they were able to shift their perspective about God and their ability to be in control of their lives they were empowered and their confidence increased instantly

Missy's Story

Missy was a 31-year-old high-level executive with a MBA running her parents company in Los Angeles, CA. Her finances were in order, she drove a Range Rover, she owned several rental properties, traveled the world with her friends, was a very beautiful woman with shoulder length hair and a gorgeous smile with beautiful teeth. She worked very hard on keeping her sexy physique and was very disciplined when it came to fasting and dieting to keep her weight down.

Missy's lifestyle was a dream life for so many women I know. However, with all that Missy had, she still did not feel complete, she didn't feel satisfied, she found it hard to keep love relationships, she did not trust many people, and she seemed detached and skeptical. Her motives were to see if she could get more from you and give you as less as possible.

Missy found me online and we began our work together. What I found was that Missy grew up Catholic but did not have a real personal spiritual connection to the Divine. She had a religion but no spirituality. When Missy came to me, it was because she thought she wanted a career change but didn't know how to tell her parents.

As we explored her reasons for seeking coaching it became clear to me that she lacked confidence and she didn't trust herself or her decisions, she was trapped in the game of wanting to make sure she didn't let her parents down. She thought getting her degrees would prove her worth, she thought running the company in the best way possible would prove her worth, she thought not getting married right away would prove her loyalty. Missy was doing all these things but didn't know who she was and didn't really know if what she wanted was ever enough. When we explored her belief system and her spiritual self-care, she did not have one; she did not understand what I was talking about, like so many.

That's when I knew her issue wasn't about her parents or her career. Missy did not have a Divine connection; therefore, she lacked confidence and personal satisfaction. This became evident when Missy stated she didn't even know how to pray or meditate and didn't understand the Bible when she read it.

Missy's first three weeks of coaching was to activate her spirit and feel the connection to the Divine. In the first week, she reported feeling awkward and sluggish with the directives I gave her. By the second week she was enjoying it. During week three she felt alive almost resuscitated. She was jovial, excited and had a sense of purpose. By week four she was a confident powerhouse. Crying with tears of joy she felt what she never felt before and that was the feeling of connectedness and like she mattered.

Missy said she was lead to travel to Turkey and release some old pain, resentment and her old scarred self. Missy realized her world was fine and that all she needed was to be connected spiritually. I remember one night we both cried in her session when she said to me, "Now I know what it means to know God and Nekisha you are the big sister I never had."

What a joy it was seeing her feeling herself as a whole person. All it took was a few simple guided solutions to get her in alignment with the divine. Missy then found a church of her choice to gather with other likeminded people to increase her faith and spiritual practices.

Missy also realized that she was ready to open herself up to love and wanted to share her life with another because she was no longer feeling lost. As the old hymn says, "Amazing grace how sweet the sound that saved a wretch like me, I once was lost but now I'm found, was blind but now I see."

Operation Reboot

The awesome thing about Operation Reboot is being educated to have the ability to make intelligent and conscious decisions about our well-being. Although it takes courage and trust to admit how we really feel on the inside, I pray that we can get to a place in our lives where we become committed to the journey and the process of transformation.

Unless we are rich on the inside, we will feel that we are never enough or have enough. We will always feel inferior, insecure and that our authentic selves are not enough.

In order to change that feeling, we must welcome a DNA reprogramming. We cannot make up for what we feel we earned but did not get, nor can we regain what we've lost. However, we can start embracing and living from a new perspective and we can reframe the story of our past. We can focus on the lessons, the inspiration and the journey from a mindset that we can transform all the things we are not happy with right here and right now rather than struggling with the pain, hurt and confusion of the past.

In the process of breaking invisible chains, you no longer have to accept your natural DNA. I have learned from my experience, that my dysfunction has a lot to do with my natural DNA which is linked to my family upbringing and having a history rooted in African American slavery. The combination of all of the above created an identity crisis with my self-worth and perception of life. However, I was able to reboot by learning to rely on my Divine connection which overpowered my previously learned unconscious programming.

I often share with my clients, as I have had to learn through many difficult experiences, that your family is not defined by who is related to you. To me, people with similar blood heritage make you related or relatives; however, FAMILY is made up of those who are sent to support, teach, guide, help, correct, push, pull and inspire you to be the best you possible.

It is not unusual to seek the approval and support of your relatives; however, from a spiritual DNA perspective, your relatives are sometimes the very people that need to be expelled from your life because of the ability they have to "break your spirit". Take a deep breath. Look around. You are part of a new spiritual family and they are always ready to be there for you.

Operation Reboot can be best described as removing a virus from our emotional computer and replacing it with a new operating system with superior antivirus software. If you ever had that happen, you know from experience that the computer runs like new.

It is faster, free of popups, and you can run each application without crashing. Romans 12:2 (NIV) from the Holy Bible states:

Do not conform any longer to the pattern of this world, but be transformed by the renewing of your mind. Then you will be able to test and approve what God's will is – his good, pleasing, and perfect will.

.

Starting today, stop looking back and start doing; use the exercises in the book to move forward. With the awareness of your spiritual DNA it will be much easier to experience your breakthrough. You will learn to connect spiritually with the Divine who adores you unconditionally. That feeling of God's presence with you creates a confidence that empowers you and gives you a deep knowing that nothing can stop you from being bold and intentional about the life you have been gifted.

Spiritual Alignment

How do we become spiritually aligned? There are three simple steps that I would like to walk you through. I live by these principles. When I feel out of control, I always go to the spiritual practices that I will explain later in this chapter.

What I found is that when we feel hopeless we think that we have no other options. However, the best thing to do is to consult our spiritual guide and be still. This protects us from feeling weak, depressed, or that we deserved the pain resulting from the situation that we experienced. When we feel like no one hears us or cares, a part of us dies. However, a breakthrough in our spirit will destroy our tendency to sabotage ourselves.

Operation Reboot will guide you out of hiding or isolation and it will help you take control of the problem. Rebooting will inspire you to activate your personal power to expose, or be honest with, yourself and others. By rebooting you will be reminded that your life does not have to consist of being trapped, chained, and afraid to love and live.

Please understand that transformation is a journey to be enjoyed and although I wish it was a simple journey, it is not. Anytime you are moving into a new paradigm, it requires you to be alert spiritually, emotionally, and mentally. This reboot is going to teach you to respond differently to life's difficulties and challenges, as well as create clearly defined boundaries

While you are rebooting, you have to discipline yourself daily, bit by bit, one day at a time. Right now, you may see yourself as being small, weak and limited in how to make changes. The way you see yourself is how you will be seen and treated. In time, you will see yourself in the Divine's own image, radiating big soulful love and power from the inside out. This practice has the power to save your life if you employ it. It has kept me here and helped me remain focused and balanced.

You will no longer carry the shame and crippling effects of your past, because I will show you what to do with them. Empowered people don't carry shame. From this day forward, no more talk about shame and struggle and woe is me! All that drama is being removed, because your spiritual connection to God is going to supersede your problems before they have a chance to manifest. You are going to be bad to the bone!

Once you master Operation Reboot people will wonder, "How is it that you live drama free and problem free?" Your answer is going to be "GOOD!" What does that mean? I realize that we all have our own belief about God and the Divine. Sometimes we use these words so much that we become desensitized to their power and meaning. Therefore, instead of referring to my divinity as God I will refer to my divinity as GOOD! When you know that Good is everywhere and Good is supporting you and Good is in you. You can't be and experience anything but Good. My spiritual DNA is that of the Good family. Allow me to be the first to welcome you home to Good.

Boot Camp for the Soul

Boot Camp for the Soul will provide you with important drills and disciplines vital to your personal growth and the maturation of your character. Your character is who you are at the core of your being. This is the person you are when no one is watching. The boot camp drills will retrain your mind, desires, and emotions to respond positively to all of life's situations. You have a new life waiting on you. It is so important that you learn the disciplines needed to stabilize your soul in Good. It is time to get it together and the only person with the authority to make it happen is you.

It would be a shame for you to read this book and not learn how to apply its teachings and strategies. I don't want you only empathizing with my life and my story; I want this information to help you create a happy ending to your story. It is time to move what we know from our head to our hearts. It is time to form new treasures. Once you go through boot camp, you will be rewarded like any good soldier. You will reap the fruit or reward based on the intensity, commitment, and passion you demonstrated during your boot camp experience.

There is no time limit on how long you should be in boot

camp. I will not mislead you and say "do this for twenty-one days" or "do that for six weeks" and you are going to be a new person. Your rewards will be based on your dedication, your achievement, and your ability to stay empowered. You will lose sleep, you will have to reread parts of this book, you will have to become intimate with your Good, and you will need to find a likeminded spiritual tribe with which to associate. To paraphrase from Joshua

1:9:*Be strong and courageous. Do not be terrified; do not be discouraged, for the Lord your Good will be with you wherever you go.*

DRILL 1: Code P.U.S.H. – E.M.

P.U.S.H. simply stands for Pray Until Something Happens, and E.M. stands for Early Meditation. The book of James 5:13a says, "Is any one of you in trouble? He should pray." Praying empties, the soul and divinely shares the issues and concerns of your heart. Praying sends verbal and energetic messaging to Good and it penetrates the universe of all that concerns you. The challenge for most of us is knowing how to pray and what to pray.

For many years I practiced the Christian Charismatic way of praying, which is either to use The Lord's Prayer (Matthew 6:9-13) or to pray in an unknown language said to be given by the Holy Spirit. In my maturity and growth, I have found the most effective prayers are the prayers that I write in the morning, sharing all that I feel I need to share.

I write until my soul feels cleansed and at peace. After my prayers, I then create a gratitude list of at least 50 things for which I am grateful. When I complete my gratitude list, I am always feeling so abundant, happy and ready for my day.

The magic that I've found in writing my prayers is that Good answers them almost immediately. If they aren't answered imme diately, Good gives me lessons to complete that prepares me for what I requested or helps me bring closure to specific issues. Now, when I pray I feel connected and heard.

Beginning each morning with early prayer is a powerful way to control your thoughts, feelings, and responses throughout the day. It is a sacrifice that requires discipline. It means you are putting Good first and making Good the priority of your day. It means you are not taking for granted that you woke up. It means that you are not preoccupied with what you didn't do the night before or what you could be doing.

You are making a statement that says you can't do anything without Good. Good is the essence of our being. When we are not connected to Good, we are not connected to ourselves; we run the risk of being powerless over situations and circumstances that may occur. Prayer creates spiritual freedom and lightens the hardship and heaviness of the soul. When spiritual fulfillment and power are missing, the soul will cry.

I love them that love me; and those that seek me early shall find me. – Proverbs 8:17 (NIV)

The more time you spend in prayer, the more you will build your prayer muscle and your supernatural blessing of confidence. The confidence that you are not alone and that Good hears you. John 5:14-15 (NIV) states:

This is the confidence we have in approaching God: that if we ask anything according to His will, He hears us. And if we know that He hears us – whatever we ask – we know that we have what we asked of Him.

In short, that means Good is on your side and will always say yes. It may not be when you want it but understand if it's Wwithin the will of Good, Good will answer with yes. I always tell

Wmy clients, that delayed does not mean denied - it just means not YET. You have more work to do.

After you have written your prayers and gratitude list, it is time to participate in Early Meditation (EM). Sit quietly with your eyes closed or using a focal point in front of you and quiet your mind. To remain still and quiet your mind chatter, you must focus on breathing in and out. Your breaths keep you conscious and quiet.

When your mind is quiet, Good can download and deposit in your spirit: your answers, your strength, your peace of mind, your courage, your confidence, your power, your patience, your desires, your inspiration and your next best steps. Good desires to be in deep communication and have a soul bond with you based on trust. However, you have to train yourself to be still and hear with your heart.

Good is always communicating with us but we don't always hear because we are busy crying, complaining, talking or stuffing our pain with placebos. Early Meditation is an amazing time and the most likely time that you will feel the powerful presence of Good. Are you ready to break your invisible chains?

Set your alarm clock to wake up thirty minutes to one hour earlier than your normal wake-up time. When it goes off, get up and get it done; put Code P.U.S.H. – E.M. to work!

The following exercise will help you make the best of Code P.U.S.H. - E.M.:

Date:____________________

Begin Time:______________**End Time:**_______________

What are you feeling?

What is the foundation of this feeling? Where did it come from?

After completing the P.U.S.H. – EM exercise, what is the result?

DRILL 2: I AM

What exactly is I AM? It is a powerful chant made of positive affirmations that I refer to as SOULFIRMATIONS. Soulfirmations are sentences that reinforce what you want to feel, manifest and observe in your life. Each chapter of this book begins with a soulfirmation and I suggest that you make some of your own, tailor-made just for you.

Chanting the words, I AM helped me take ownership of my personal power, which I refer to as my goddess power, and create a new paradigm through which Good could thrive without interruption. When challenges or fears arise, Good manifests Itself in a surreal way so that I can handle it all because of who I AM. My soul stays firm in knowing who I AM and I AM able to remind my soul, with the strength from my spirit, that I AM a friend of Good and ONLY Good supports me regardless of what I see or feel. It is all Good and for my good.

This is when I teach my clients that their reaction keeps them perpetuating the same drama and hardships they want to release. The best and most effective way to move forward is by focusing on the feelings you want to be your dominate feelings, which come from the right side of your soul. The right side of your soul is your Spiritual DNA but I am going to refer to it as love and goodness. Therefore, use I AM to get you there.

This is a drill that needs to be done at least twice a day. In fact, I believe that you should place I AM on every mirror in your house and on the rearview mirror of your car. Once you get there, it may feel fake, it may feel unrealistic and that is because the left side of soul is your EGO, which attributes to your fears. For the purposes of this book we will refer to the left side as fear. Fear is trying to prove to you that what it offers is more real and comfortable than where you want to be.

Fear does not want to die, so in order to be gentle with yourself through this process you have to talk to yourself and be conscience you will have bouts of resistance and fear.

Positive Soul-Talk Formula*:*

"Thank you, soul, for taking care of me the best way you could from the left side. I am now emerging into a more powerfully aligned person and that requires me to stay on the right side of my soul. The proof that this is my new state of mind, I remember all the times I used the right side of my soul and the results were phenomenal. When I use the left side of my soul, the results left me feeling inadequate, hurt, afraid and desperate. Thank you, soul, for shifting to the right side because I can't be pitiful and powerful at the same time. I love you."

It's always more powerful to create your own I AM but until you can get to that place I have listed mine for you to borrow. Say 'I AM' while looking into the mirror in order to penetrate your soul with the following statement:

1. Beautiful & Abundant
2. Honest & Bold
3. Prosperous & Generous
4. Respected & Honored
5. Radiant & Influential
6. Peaceful & Loving
7. Confident & Skilled in my work.
8. Valuable & Intelligent
9. Sexy & Sensual
10. Significant & Wanted

11. Powerful & Esteemed
12. Healthy & Vibrant
13. Resilient & Supported
14. Complete & Whole
15. Full of the good life & Soaring in my hearts desire's
16. Honest & Aligned to my highest Good
17. Living at a high vibration & Patient
18. Learning & Growing in Good
19. Meeting my needs & Full of passion
20. Emotionally stable & Mentally strong
21. Quick to listen, Slow to speak & Slow to become angry
22. Humble & Enjoying my ideal image and body weight

DRILL 3: Saturate

Drill Saturate creates a safe place, a peaceful place, and a place where it is easy to feel the Good presence. It helps soothe the spirit and it encourages the soul. What exactly is Drill Saturate? It is filling your home, car, office, or favorite place with peaceful music, motivational teachings, symbols that remind you to be at peace and visions of your life as you want to manifest it. It could be a library of different subject matters that you want to achieve mastery in. Saturate can be a bucket list of things you want to do or accomplish and you decide to just do it.

The whole idea is to keep your environment in alignment with your I AM. The more aligned you are with your NEW TRUTH the easier it will be for the fear to find its final resting place. This drill helps me change the atmosphere of my environment. I practice it when negativity seems to be present or something just doesn't feel right.

By saturating your whole atmosphere, you will improve your prayer, praise, understanding, and wisdom about your new life. When there is peace and understanding, it is hard for the Boogie Man and other negative forces to dwell. You want to constantly allow peaceful, blissful influences into your spirit while you are sleeping as well as while you are awake. What goes into your soul via your eyes and ears will often dictate you will react or respond to situations and circumstances.

Your environment should be beautiful and free of any hoarding activity, dirt, broken things, old un-useful items. It should be free of hurtful memories and meaningless items. Everything around you should have meaning, be beneficial and evoke the Good in you. Before you saturate your environment, start with a good cleaning and smudging.

What is smudging?

Smudging is the common name given to the Native American tradition known as the Sacred Smoke Bowl Blessing. This is a powerful spiritual cleansing technique which calls upon the spirits of various sacred plants to drive away negative energy and to restore balance to an individual, a group, a space, or all three. This tradition has been a part of the spirituality of Native Americans for thousands of years and now this cleansing ritual is available to anyone who is willing to give it a try. The ritual is very simple and very empowering. You don't need a lot of expensive equipment to start doing it in your own home.

Smudging allows you to wash away all the emotional and spiritual negativity that gathers in your body and your space over time. It's a little bit like taking a spiritual shower! The effects of smudging can be very effective, often banishing stress almost instantly and providing energy and peace. Smudging can also help your body and space to adjust to the healing rhythms of the seasonal cycle. More than anything, smudging can turn your space and your body into a peaceful, beautiful temple in which you can rejuvenate yourself and find happiness.

Any sort of fragrant, medicinal herb can be used in smudging. Some tribes use cedar as a way of carrying prayers up to heaven. Lavender can provide a calming and soothing energy in a chaotic situation. Bundles of sage are the most popular. **White sage** *(Salvia apiana)*, also known as **Sacred Sage**, is burned as a traditional way to cleanse away negative or lingering energy from objects, people or from a room. These herbs can be found in holistic / organic stores or ordered online.

How to Smudge

The ritual for smudging is simple. Just walk about the perimeter of the room, giving special attention to the corners and the places behind doors. You can also fan the smoke throughout the room with a large feather. If you are amenable to the notion, you should state a prayer of gratitude for the cleansing and keep in mind your intention of removing any negatively inclined energy from the area during the ritual.

This is also a great time to do your prayer to release fear and chant your "I AM". I usually will smudge whenever I feel stagnant or ready to make a major life shift. It always leaves me feeling relieved, peaceful and in control.

DRILL 4: Identify Your Love Tribe

Let the wise listen and add to their learning, and let the discerning get guidance – Proverbs 1:5.

Identifying your Love Tribe helps you become accountable. Being accountable is being wise. Sound wisdom will keep your soul out of trouble. We all benefit from someone who can help us accelerate our growth and point out to us where we could use some fine tuning and adjustments. No one ever becomes a master without having someone that is able to pass the torch of life to them. If you're ever going to be great, you must first be in the presence of someone that holds the wisdom of what greatness is.

Most people who are trying to overcome emotional challenges, disappointments, or tragedies will go to therapy. Therapy is fine, as long as the morals of the therapist match yours. Therapists are safe because they allow you to cleanse your soul and provide encouragement, solutions, and opportunities to help you grow. However, I am an advocate of life coaching because it helps you understand your limiting habits, while challenging you to create a strategy and plan for the future you want and desire. I believe we all need to put our energy toward the future and lay the past to rest. Take what you need, but lay it to rest. Nurture the possibility of having it all.

Don't nurture the pain or the hurt that has kept you from what you have always wanted. A life coach can help you do just that. In fact, a life coach just like me is the best route to accomplish that. You know I am laughing at this shameless promotion; however, if you are enjoying this book but want to join my Love Tribe so that you can embody the wisdom being provided in this book, feel free to join my Facebook group at: www.facebook.com/groups/readywomanlovecircle. This group is for women only is private and free of charge.

Beware of Psychic Help

Some people have a tendency to go to psychics, palm readers, and astrologists. **(WARNING:** The messages they speak are not always representing Good.) Although they are gifted in being sensitive to spiritual matters, you must be careful of their influence. Find an intuitive that you feel comfortable with and that comes highly recommended from someone you know. Some operate at lower consciousness levels which is associated to your fears. Therefore, they can be manipulating and evoke fear.

I am intuitive and when you are psychic it's easy to be drawn to that energy, as well as when your life is such a mess or you have a lot of anxiety. Although it can be a great source of wisdom and help, I strongly suggest you be led by prayer and meditation not fear and desperation. When I coach my clients, I always tell them at this point you are in Intensive Care and for 30 days you must refrain from activities that may conflict with the guidance of Good.

I had a psychic addiction. There was a time that I spent thousands of dollars consulting with psychics. The end result was that I was more confused and broke. I am proud to say that for the past seven years, I have found safety and Good wisdom in the co-pastor of one of my former churches and having hired both my own personal life coaches and business coaches. Sometimes there is that one special angel that knows you so well and always know what to do to get your soul out of the critical care unit.

Spiritual Mentoring

I have a spiritual mentor. Someone who speaks wisdom to my spirit. From the very first day I met Pastor Valda Hilton, affectionately called Pastor V, she has been an inspiration to me. When I receive what she says, I grow! She's more than just my spiritual mentor; she's my spiritual mother.

I remember being a single parent and having difficulty making ends meet. I thought the answer was getting a second job. However, after sharing this with Pastor V, she told me that she did not believe that it was good for me to work several jobs and be robbed of the time needed to parent my child. She told me that if I continued to be faithful and pray for the answer, and be open to do whatever Good wanted me to do, the way for me to overcome this obstacle would become clear.

Although I trusted her wisdom, I knew that my current income was not compatible with my bills. In addition to that, I was homeless and living in the basement of one of the other single moms of our church. I had two choices: either do as Pastor V said or do the logical thing and get a part-time job. I decided to do as my spiritual mentor stated and continued to pray, pay tithes to my church and believe that the answer would come. It did.

As a graduate intern, I developed a spirituality curriculum for a program called Women's Drug Court in Cincinnati. The administrator of the program contacted me and asked me to teach the curriculum to her staff, as well as provide group counseling to the residents for two hours a week. She said that she would pay me the general contractor fee, which put an additional five hundred dollars a month in my pocket.

The best part was that I didn't lose any time with my daughter because she was at choir rehearsal during the time I was counseling and teaching. It didn't feel like work because I was doing what I love to do, which is to help people—especially women—persevere. Soon after that, I landed another job in child protective services, which increased my income by ten thousand dollars annually.

I followed sound, mature advice and I got powerful results. Everyone needs a spiritual mentor. Oprah confesses to standing on the shoulders of the late beloved Dr. Maya Angelou; I stood on the shoulders of Pastor V. Who are you standing on the shoulders of? Better yet, are you living in such an aligned way that someone could stand on your shoulders?

Filling the Gaps of the Past

Even though I didn't get what I needed from my biological mother, Good made sure that my spiritual mother provided me with what I needed to keep growing and progressing.

Some women will say they don't trust other women, but that is a self-worth and spirituality issue. When you are spiritually discerning, you will know who has your best interest and who doesn't. So, lay down the excuses, become discerning, and give yourself credit for trying to figure out a way to protect what is in your heart. Remember that following sound, spiritual wisdom will help you be more open and willing to experience freedom and not fear.

I went through a season when I felt like my world was crumbling. I couldn't find the strength to help myself. I began questioning Good. Just when I was going numb from feeling abandoned by my business partners and feeling rejected by some women I thought loved me, Pastor V called. Unaware of where I was spiritually, she sent me a ticket to come and spend some time with her. Pastor V and her husband, Bishop Hilton, opened their door and allowed me to make their home my restorative place.

Their home was a spiritual hospital for me because my soul was crying and I needed reinforcement to reboot my spiritual alignment. I learned from this experience that it is important to have a restorative place for the soul.

Classy Communication

During my visit, I was not allowed to feel sorry for myself or play the victim. Pastor V made me go into the special room she and her husband, the Bishop, had prepared for me where I could use my Boot Camp principles on myself. She gave me lessons and instructed me to research and meditates on them. Then she would quiz me on what I had read and understood. She prayed with me and made me go to church with her and the Bishop morning, noon, and night.

When she was done helping me feed my spirit, she talked to me about what I refer to with my clients as "Classy Communication", despite what I was feeling. This woman-to-woman talk didn't make me feel good, but it was essential for the purpose of ensuring that I sustained healthy relationships. Pastor V talked to me about communicating from love not from feeling like someone owed me or my anger and hurt.

That kind of communication never resolves or helps anyone or anything. When you speak from fear, it is the little hurt girl trying to find significance and value. However, Pastor V instilled in me that as a Woman it is important to already know your significance and values. She also taught me how to communicate when boundaries have been crossed, not because of hurt feelings. She reminded me that no one is responsible for my feelings or how I perceived the events in my life.

Pastor V helped me realize that as you are on your life path, there will be times when you have to ask for forgiveness, even when you feel you haven't done anything wrong. Some battles are not worth fighting and there are times when you have to lead others to the path of what is right by demonstrating control and restraint through Classy Communication.

Feelings Conveyed via Communication

In my relationships, I found it challenging to share my disappointment and grievances with others, so my way of sharing my hurt was to act it out. To give you some examples, I got a huge kick out of slamming phones down without saying goodbye. I wanted to be rude and leave the other person hanging on, feeling disrespected.

I also would not return phone calls, avoid events so I wouldn't have to be around someone specific, and act on my childish impulses. I'd get a kick out of cursing and causing emotional harm if I felt like I was being rejected or abandoned. If I thought for a moment that you were trying to attack me, I would use any weapons in my arsenal to verbally degrade you. It was just how I used to protect myself from pain.

However, after that weekend with Pastor V, I learned that my way was not the mature way and that everyone has feelings. In fact, if I wanted to be a great leader, I had to get myself together and not worry about what other people were doing. I couldn't be in control of what they did, but I could be in control of what I did. If I wanted to have great friends and loyal relationships, I had to be a great friend and loyal. I had to spiritually discern when it was not the right season or time and just be a woman and say so.

Pastor V also taught me how to talk to people so that they would feel good about following me and being in my personal space. She reminded me that self-evaluation is critical before pointing the finger and shifting the blame. She helped me see that I was important to Good, I had no choice but to grow up and be the woman I'm supposed to be regardless of how others acted toward me. In truth, Pastor V held the same mirror up to me that I would hold up to others.

That reflection in the mirror showed me the emotionally and spiritually underdeveloped woman that I was at the core. She explained to me that to be effective in my life's purpose, I needed to accept that I was special to Good and I am being held accountable for my life. The seeds that I was sowing prior to this weekend with her were seeds of anger, mistrust, and living a lie. I was giving advice that I wasn't willing to follow.

Pastor V scolded and nurtured me with love. She didn't judge me, and whenever I felt her presence, I no longer struggled with my identity, my feelings, or my worth. That weekend was the catalyst for this book. It changed me forever! As a matter of fact, I walk away a changed woman after each time we get together. I truly love and admire Pastor V, and I am extremely thankful for her entering my life when she did.

I've had so many angels in my Love Tribe and they all seem to fill in the gaps of my life that were missing because I had abusive mother and an absent father. These angels are Goodly influences in my life. Like Pastor V, they have never allowed me to regress and continue to push me toward progress. They give me books and assignments to keep me focused and whenever I'm sponsoring an event or doing something special they support me. People like this are rare but shows you that Good is always present even if it's not in the form you THINK it should be.

My spiritual family doesn't replace my biological family, but they are the voice of reason, support, and wisdom that I trust. Their guidance and opinions mean so much to me, and my growth and happiness mean so much to them. Having them as spiritual examples in my life helps me stay focused and grounded, and it keeps me from opening the door to the pain of my past and expecting my mother and other family members to give me what they can't. They keep me from feeling confused and lost for even expecting my biological family to help me in areas that they have not healed in themselves.

My spiritual DNA is taking care of what my biological DNA could not. I believe that blood connection makes you related but the love and support connection makes you family. You cannot make this journey of transformation without a Love Tribe. Find yours today and start by joining my women only free online love tribe https://www.facebook.com/groups/ReadyWomanLoveCircle/

The Good Can

Sometimes I get blocked when I have money issues or there is a difficult goal I want to accomplish. I used to cry and obsess over it and feel sorry for myself after having prayed and still have not received an answer. I would panic, become anxious and have many restless nights. Those reactions do not demonstrate faith and is not how to access personal power. It is also does not demonstrate freedom from invisible chains.

A wise woman used to remind me, "When the student is ready, the teacher will appear." Finally, when I was ready to stop worrying and obsessing so much about everything I did not know the answer to, an old friend told me about The Good Can. Here's how it works:

Take a used, empty food can from the grocery store. On the outside of the can write the words "My Good Can". Place the can in a place that's considered to be sacred and used as a prayer alter. On index cards, write down each challenging issue, concerns, and blocks. Then turn the issue over to Good and say, "Good Can," and drop each card into the can and leave it ALONE. Don't think about it, don't pray over it just give it to the Good Can and let the can hold your burdens.

Feeling Light

Initially, my Good Can was filled with challenges but all my burdens were being lifted from my mind and energy. The miracle about the Good Can is that it truly removes the problem, and I don't have to deal with it. Furthermore, when I least expect it, the solution to the issue will manifest with speed because I'm not nursing the problem but trusting that GOOD CAN. Then I write the date I realized the problem was taken care of on the outside of the can.

The dates on the outside of the can serve as a reminder of all the situations that Good has taken care of for me because I believed. Finally, I remove the issue from my Good Can and throw it away. What usually happens is my Good Can becomes empty, proving that GOOD CAN! Further creating actual evidence to the fear that it's work is done!

Step 3: Reboot Your Spirit

Chapter 3 Expansion Exercises: "Rebooting Your Spirit"

I'm sure you now fully understand why it's time for you to become a master in "Rebooting Your Spirit." That is where the power to break your invisible chains resides.

What important concepts have you learned from this chapter that have been a major Hot Dayum moments/ Aha?

____

____

____

When will you begin to practice the drills?

____

____

____

Why do you need to practice all three drills?

____

____

____

Make a list of at least three possible spiritual mentors that you could ask to help you stay accountable. Call them today and tell them what you need from them. Ask them if they would be willing to support you. I hope I'm one of them (hint, hint).

____

____

____

Create your GOOD CAN within the next 48 hours if you believe that Good Can. Make a list of what will go in the can so you don't forget and you can get rid of those things weighing you down.

________________________ ________________________

________________________ ________________________

________________________ ________________________

________________________ ________________________

________________________ ________________________

Write down three people for whom you will give this book to so you can create your Love Tribe.

____

____

____

I AM Story Board

The more you saturate your environment with the new you and your new feelings, the more natural it becomes. This assignment is to create your I AM story board.

1. Get a poster board, scissors, magazine, paint, markers, glue, tape…etc.

2. Create a huge circle representing the Sun, the source of all energy and life. In the circle write the words, I AM (or you can copy the example on the following page).

3. Create different size sun rays extending from the sun with your positive soulfirmations about who you are NOW and will always be. You can use color coding to represent different areas of your life (see example from a client).

Frame your work or place it on an easel and put it somewhere that creates significance and you can marvel at your beauty everyday…I AM is YOU!

I AM

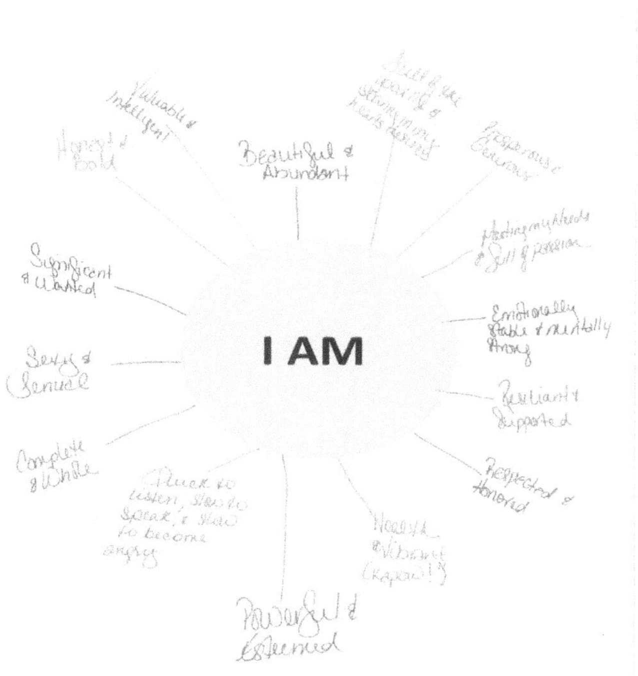

Chapter 4
Rewrite Your Story

Soulfirmation:

"I Am the star in my own film. I am the producer, director and author. I create amazing roles for myself with ease."

Denying Doesn't Heal It

I was employed as a social worker for over 15 years. I was trained to recognize the dysfunction in families that cause heightened risk or harm that result in domestic violence, child abuse and poverty. A typical family on my case load would be a drug dependent mother, a child who had been abused physically and/or sexually by a family member, or children in alternative schools due to behavioral problems. Most of these families were African-American, usually headed by a single parent with more than one child, and living on government assistance in government subsidized housing.

As a general routine, I would do a gene-o-gram on the primary person in my caseload. A gene o gram is a picture chart of that person's family history, including crises and major family changes, the notation of risky behaviors or lifestyles, and any significant information that helps the social worker or therapist get an accurate picture of the family system. This is sometimes the fastest and least intrusive way for social worker to get the information needed to make an accurate assessment of what is and was going on in the family.

This information helps to create a unique treatment plan and appropriate intervention to reduce crises and avoid serious consequences of dysfunctional or risky behavior. What I repeatedly saw was that my primary client was only repeating the life of one or both of her parents, with only slight variations. One of the other significant factors I noticed was that all of my clients believed they were giving their children a better life than they had experienced growing up.

To complicate matters further, there was a recurring element of misfortune that could be traced back to the parents and grandparents, such as rape, molestation, physical abuse, partying all the time, or not spending enough time with the children. In addition, the affected child or children always felt somehow neglected, unnoticed, burdened down or shamed.

Of course, this prompted me to look at my own family. Until this point, I hated my mother and blamed her for not loving me. I blamed her for not treating me right. I blamed her for not supporting me. However, after completing a personal assessment of my family I realized that my mother was only doing and demonstrating what she had been taught. She could not help it; she did not know any other way.

As a matter of fact, even when I think about all the terrible things she said to my brothers and me, I'm grateful that we were not the direct offspring of her parents. It made sense. My mother truly thought she was giving us a much better life than the one her parents gave her. Yet she was repeating what she had experienced in a different way. She was demonstrating to us how she felt on the inside—unloved and out of control.

I didn't know a lot of details about my family history during this time but I realized from the little I did know that both sides of my family were very similar and there were things that were not talked about. The ironic thing was that those things that were not talked about were the cycles of dysfunction that kept getting repeated. These were issues the family didn't like to talk about, although some of it leaked out during family gatherings or arguments. This was the stuff we had kept swept under the rug to give the illusion that we were perfect.

These were issues that when discussed or questioned, everyone either got quiet or went into denial. Because we did not take a proactive approach and discuss it, something called a 'curse' had been inadvertently passed on from generation to generation. Analyzing the facts and developing the skill of analyzing the past are key to being able to move forward with breaking invisible chains. In business, I have devoted several years of my life to understanding that an analysis of trends, both past and present, is necessary to create momentum and increase profitability.

When I started my first business in network marketing, what I was able to create and do well created a profitable future; however, the things I ignored, denied and neglected led me to many failed attempts at business success. There is no way you can obtain desired outcomes for your future without examining the past realistically from different viewpoints.

I used to work for a network marketing business and there was one particular consultant that I remember, Sherry Fields. Sherry became the company's first person to receive one million dollars in commissions and eventually she earned the nickname of "Money Maker." The "Money Maker" used to say in private coaching sessions with me and in various business trainings that she made a habit of sleeping with her organizational genealogy.

This meant she studied her numbers and activity closely day and night. She familiarized herself with her team to the point that she knew how to reward them and she knew what inspired them to become some of the company's top producers. Sherry knew the seasons her teams did their best work and when they needed the most support. She knew this because she studied the trends and history of her past team activity.

The rigorous skill of analyzing her team's activity led to the Money Maker's substantial success in the business. This is the same methodology I used to identify the gaps and challenges of generational disadvantages that seemed to plague my family lineage.

I used the gene-o-gram I mentioned earlier to track the identified patterns of crises and misfortunes that interfered with my quality of life. Before you can right the wrong, you must understand and admit to what is wrong! Listen to the history because it matters and denying it does not make it disappear.

What I heard when I listened

Our feelings influence the way we perceive events. Those feelings are learned from the examples demonstrated by our environment and inherited from our relatives. Feelings are transferrable and the meaning we apply to life's events are directly influenced by the way our parents parented. Many of our parents worked so hard to give us a "better" life but what they meant by better was often a financially secure future. As we are chosen to break invisible chains we have to shift what we term as a "better" life to create a better "emotional" life.

Our parents worked so diligently to ensure that we had the material substance but not the emotional substance. In fact, that is often the reason why my clients, and myself included, have "things" that are considered symbols of success but we often feel empty. That is why we find ourselves in hurtful broken relationships and no matter how much we thought we had, it didn't equate to confidence and how we valued others more than ourselves.

Our families gave us their brokenness, their pain and despair. As a result, we spend a lifetime trying not to go insane and to rid ourselves of all this heaviness, disappointment and mistakes that we inherited from their feelings and behaviors.

In the first sessions with my clients, I always have them tell their story and be heard because for so long they have had to keep it a secret as to not hurt anyone or bring shame among themselves or their family. However, the shame, confusion and resentment lives in us all because we place our "family" desires in a higher regard than our sanity.

So, what if you were raped, molested, or just felt that you couldn't appear weak in your family. What if you were the one that didn't get into any trouble and stayed out of the way so you were not a burden to your family? What if you were the one that was blamed for everything that went wrong? Your subconscious mind is sending out those feelings because you were raised in the environment with those feelings; therefore, life attracted events and situations to perpetuate those same familiar feelings. There is always an exception to the rule, but if you are reading this book, it is likely that you are not the exception and neither was I.

After you acknowledge the source of the pain your job is to rewrite the script of your story from a perception and feelings of strength. When you rewrite your story, you become better able to not project the patterns and energy of the old story but of your new one. We tell our minds what to believe and I found the quickest way to healing is reassign the belief and rewire the feelings. If you don't, you will not be able to thrive in confidence and you too will pass on the dysfunction of damaged past.

How Do You Rewrite the Story?

How do you need to rewrite your story? Take some time and tell your story the way you know it and put it in a journal, tell it through video, write your book or tell your story through poetry or music. It doesn't matter how you tell your story but it matters that you do. Your voice matters and although we are a product of our upbringing, we don't have to be powerless over it.

We are the co-creators of our lives and through the power of story telling you can change your emotional state, response and triggers from the left side of your soul to the right side. You will then have the power to give your children, nieces and nephews a truly "better" life. The examples below show how these women rewrote their stories.

Emily

Emily was raped in college. She felt shamed, she was blamed, and she was told to keep it a secret because no one would believe her. Although the rape happened and psychologically it made her feel powerless, ugly and ashamed, she rewrote her story. She realized that just because she was victimized she didn't have to own it, so she said that a man was so infatuated with her and he was too afraid of rejection so he took her body without permission.

This situation taught her to be stronger and more aware of her surroundings. She took self-defense courses, assertiveness training, and learned to trust her instincts. She created a ministry to support other female rape survivors. In addition, she became a motivational speaker by telling her story, which gave her extra money to enjoy her hobbies and vacations with ease.

Annie

Annie was mistreated and made to work harder as a child because she was darker in skin complexion than her siblings. She was often yelled at, given leftovers and was not allow to have the fun the other kids were having. Annie agreed that just because she was singled out and mistreated that she didn't have to own that story or those feelings.

So, Annie rewrote her story and stated, the reason she is so amazingly strong and a top executive in her company is because as a child she owned being unique from others and when they were playing she learned the skills necessary to sacrifice fun for work and do the important things. She now interprets the yelling from her grandmother as the ability to withstand different emotions that people exhibit when they are under pressure and seem to can't get their needs met. She is able to empathize and be a problem solver with quick solutions.

Children Learn What They Live

There is a poem I remember learning as a young child called "Children Learn What They Live." Maybe you to know it, but please allow me to reacquaint you with Dorothy Law Nolte's insights.

If children live with criticism, they learn to condemn.
If children live with hostility, they learn to fight.
If children live with fear, they learn to be apprehensive.
If children live with pity, they learn to feel sorry for themselves.
If children live with ridicule, they learn to feel shy.
If children live with jealousy, they learn to feel envy.
If children live with shame, they learn to feel guilty.
If children live with encouragement, they learn confidence.
If children live with tolerance, they learn patience.
If children live with praise, they learn appreciation.
If children live with acceptance, they learn to love.
If children live with approval, they learn to like themselves.
If children live with recognition, they learn it is good to have a goal.
If children live with sharing, they learn generosity.
If children live with honesty, they learn truthfulness.
If children live with fairness, they learn justice.
If children live with kindness and consideration, they learn respect.
If children live with security, they learn to have faith in themselves and in those about them.

If children live with friendliness, they learn the world is a nice place in which to live.

As you read what I know of my family, you will be able to see that Ms. Nolte's speculation has a lot of validity because truly I learned what I lived.

Breaking the Silence

By the time my maternal grandfather, Pappi, was five years old, death had taken both of his parents. He went from household to household, living with various older siblings, and at one point, he was allegedly severely physically abused by his brother- in-law, who was also physically violent to his wife, Pappi's sister. He was extremely handsome and he eventually became a star athlete and a Baptist preacher. As a result, years later he developed an undiagnosed dual personality.

One was charming and giving to the point where he provided for his family at all costs. However, he had a dark side. He was an alcoholic and he was extremely violent and abusive toward his wife and children. His mood was very unpredictable. This affected my mother so deeply that she also became mentally unstable. She was pretty, charming, and witty, and she loved to be around people and in church. However, she was degrading, physically abusive, and she attracted inappropriate relationships with married men who were mostly preachers.

I don't know much about Mama Jay, my maternal grandmother, except that her skin was darker than of all her siblings and was oftentimes mistreated by her paternal step-grandmother, who was a preacher's wife. She would sometimes tell me how she didn't like spending time at Big Mama's (my great-great grandmother) house because she was so mean and verbally abusive.

I also know that she may have had big dreams, because she used to tell me that she wished she had attended college, but she chose to get married and have a family. A quick assessment of Mama Jay shows that she was very negative and critical but she made up for it by always attempting to put out family fires. She was not in her comfort zone unless she was investigating some family drama or using the money she worked long and hard for to bail family members out of embarrassing situations.

My father was run out of Tennessee, his place of origin, for his extreme promiscuity and violent temper. The rumor was that he had raped a woman, and he was told to leave the state or spend the rest of his life in jail. Up until that point, he had always bragged about how many children he created, which he attributed to his great looks and athletic physique.

All of that was a cover-up for the empty void he felt as a result of being made to believe that he and his older brother were abandoned by their mother, who I affectionately called Mama Maggie, my paternal grandmother. Mama Maggie, who is now deceased but who had taught me so much about life, always told me—even in her dying days— that she had not abandoned her children.

As a matter of fact, she was the sole individual who helped me make up my mind to take my daughter to college with me. "No matter what, keep your baby with you!" she warned. I had no idea the passion and conviction in her voice was due to the pain she experienced from having her children taken away from her.

Her oldest son, my Uncle Jesse, was taken from her, and my father was falsely adopted by an aunt and uncle who said they would care for him temporarily while my grandmother made a new home in Ohio for herself and her children. Mama Maggie admitted to living the fast life, one that consisted of running around with all the wrong men for financial purposes and having a good time drinking and partying. One day she became sick and tired of that life and the mistreatment by her husband, my father's biological dad. She decided to leave Chattanooga, Tennessee, and start a new life in Ohio.

She planned to get her children and bring them to Ohio to live with her after getting herself together. Well, that never happened because my father's uncle and aunt filed charges, accusing her of abandoning him. My father's aunt could not bear children, so she wanted my dad as her own. My father's older brother, Uncle Jesse, had a different father, whose family took over the care and custody of him.

Occasionally, throughout Uncle Jesse's life, my grandmother would hear news or be told through gossip where Uncle Jesse was and where he was living, but there was never any further contact between them. My grandmother died with a broken heart because of the mistake she made of leaving her children. The one thing she wanted most was to see her oldest son again but he was not found until a year after she transitioned.

My grandmother carried depression, rejection, the pain that she didn't get to raise her boys, couldn't keep a husband, and only had a few good friends to her grave. Nevertheless, she made the best of her life and found refuge and strength through going to church, her unwavering faith in God, and being an unofficial foster parent to so many children in the community. She never missed Sunday school or regular church service and during the week she would play her piano and sing her favorite songs to soothe, in my professional opinion, her crying soul.

I assume, my mother raised me out of fear because when she looked at me she saw herself and she didn't want me to follow in her footsteps. Instead of choosing to learn how to communicate effectively without pushing me away and damaging my spirit, she chose to pass down to me what was done to her. By doing this, she made me believe I was the worst abomination our family had ever seen.

My pregnancy was a huge disappointment to the family. At first, I didn't tell anyone. I was good at keeping things to myself, they didn't find out that my daughter was coming until I was already seven and a half months. When they found out, they wanted to get rid of the baby and sweep what I had done under the rug. I know you're wondering the same thing everyone else is: How was I able to live with my mother every day without her discovering that I was pregnant? Well, you will have to ask her that question! I lived the next six years with a scarlet letter on my chest. However, mine wasn't an "A", because I wasn't an adulterer; it was an "S" for Stupid.

On my twenty-first birthday, my mother decided to share her family secret with me. I guess what had been swept under the rug needed to be cleaned up and I was the recipient of her baring soul. It went something like this: "Nekisha, I've been so jealous of what you have been able to accomplish in your life. I didn't have the courage to do what you've done. But I want to let you know that I'm sorry for making you feel bad for getting pregnant when you did. I got pregnant at fourteen, too, and your grandfather beat me so bad I had a miscarriage... and I was about six months along." She also went on to share with me that she was sexually abused by her uncle and had never told a soul.

So, I don't blame my mother for anything except for not being aware that she had allowed the same thing that had been done to her to be done to me. After that confession, I learned that Mama Jay allegedly gotten pregnant as a teenager but kept having abortions until she turned eighteen and finally decided to have my mother. Ten months after that, my aunt, who I call Auntie, was born. I also eventually found out that Mama Maggie was just a teenager when she got pregnant.

I began to see the pattern that was alive and well in my genealogy—ignore the dysfunction and it will go away. That is so far from the truth. If you tell the truth, you disarm the fear of the circumstance. More intervention can take place when the truth is known. The sins of the mother and father are less likely to be visited upon by their children and each generation will not repeat issues and mistakes of their ancestors.

Almost everything I have experienced—sexual abuse, physical abuse, promiscuity, depression, anger—and the list goes on and on— did not start with me; I'm just the first one who recognized and found the courage to talk about it, give it a name, and work like hell to break it. Curses are curses to those who live their lives unconsciously. But success must be deliberate and planned. That is why this book is a part of my unfolding, and the outward acknowledgment that my lineage will no longer be accepting of whatever happens... we will be proactive in creating the life we desire and deserve. All this hurt and pain is not going to be for nothing. It had a purpose and here I am to set the rest of us free.

Residue of American Slavery

I heard an intriguing sermon in church, called Generational Curses, that explained the phenomenon that we discussed earlier about families repeating unhealthy patterns and cycles. I learned that generational curses are predisposed destructive patterns, cycles, and plagues inherited from our ancestors. If the curses are not stopped, they can affect one generation after the next until Jesus comes back.

The curses affect how we perceive ourselves and the world in which we live. They keep poverty, struggle, domestic violence, child abuse, mental illness, teen pregnancy, health related diseases, and alcohol and drug abuse alive in each generation. In order to find the root of most curses, we sometimes have to look back at least five generations.

Five Generations of Curses

Some black Americans who are doing well in America usually don't like to hear this, and there are many who are ignorant to it, but a lot of what we do and believe is nothing more than residue from slavery. Going back five generations in my family revealed the mentality and behaviors my black ancestors learned during slavery. When I was a little girl, it seemed as though that period in time was so long ago. After I got older, I realized that Harriet Tubman died in the early 1900's and I was born about seventy and some odd years later, so you do the math.

There are so many patterns our current generation possess today that are similar to the patterns our ancestors had during slavery and it leads me to believe it is the invisible chains that have caused us to repeat these patterns. Although we are no longer on plantations, we continue to involuntarily create conditions for ourselves that our ancestors were once forced to endure.

For starters, slaves were taught to survive and not thrive. Sometimes survival meant doing whatever they had to do to please the master to avoid punishment or being separated from family members. However, the family was often broken up and destroyed because of feelings of resentment by the males toward the females for having sexual relations with the master or whoever the master deemed appropriate. The masters made it hard for the black family institution to survive.

Slave families were often broken up and sold to other plantations near and far. The men would sometimes be allowed week end passes to see their families if their masters permitted it. There is a correlation between the weekend pass during slavery—from Saturday night to Sunday night—and the term booty call of today, which is so popular.

The booty call of today simply means the fellow comes to the woman for sexual intercourse but has no conviction to marry her or make the relationship binding by marriage. This is a strong indication of the frequently disregarded institution of family and lack of commitment in today's culture. During the booty call during American slavery, babies were created, and these visits meant an increase in the slave population, which was pure profit for the master who owned the woman.

It didn't matter to the master if the father was there or not, because it was the mother who had to nurture the baby and carry it to work with her in the fields; so, the paternity of the child was unimportant. Could this be from where the saying "Mama's baby, Daddy's maybe" was derived? Needless to say, slave children were regularly deprived of a father's influence.

If there were men on the same plantation, they suffered so much humiliation, torture, and punishment that real demonstration of true manhood was scarce. The model of manhood came from the master. And now, today, we are still suffering from the effects of what we learned during slavery; lots of men are not taking responsibility for their children, and we have to now send out the Child Support police to remind him that his child needs his influence and his money. Additionally, too many are violent toward their significant other in the name of getting respect and instilling fear.

The children in my scope of work are growing up in imbalanced environments, where the punishment is heavy and the nurturing is too light. Consequently, there are so many teens out of control today because that is how they feel. The drug culture is prevalent everywhere and women are having several babies with different fathers because they want love. We continue to teach bondage to our children and their children, but without intervention the problem gets worse. As a result, we are holding in our pain, treating the symptoms with self-destruction, and running away from the responsibility of breaking invisible chains.

Slaves survived off of scraps and leftovers. They lived in horrible conditions and had no rights whatsoever. Unless they were very determined and strong willed, they accepted these conditions because that was the life they were given and they were grateful for even that. Now there are ghettos and generations of families who still suffer from the curse of not expecting much and getting by on handouts.

For some of us, the ghetto is our culture and surviving to make it out of the ghetto is like a mantra. We should be asking ourselves, "Why are we in the ghetto? What is wrong?" No matter how much opportunity has been given or programs created for self-sufficiency, it seems like it is not enough. We still behave as though we are in bondage. Our bodies may have been freed from slavery, but in many cases the residue has us still teaching the institution of slavery to our children.

Oftentimes, those of us who devalue individuals living in the ghettos pass judgment and say they are lazy, trifling, and looking for handouts. We forget that even during slavery there were three different mindsets of slaves. There were the ones who believed that the 'Promised Land' was after death, so why rock the boat? Then there were the ones who believed that one day some miracle would change their situation, and they would keep praying and believing in God for better times. And finally, there were the slaves who, although they prayed, understood that if they didn't take action – like run away, plan a revolt, or learn to read and write – their situation would never change.

This book is for those ready to move to a new place, free from complacency and repeating the same mistakes of the past. This book is for those who have the courage to be without the crises, drama, and self-sabotaging situations that hinder the ability to live a life you love. There is a direct correlation between the three different mindsets of the slave and the mindsets of our current generation.

We have those who live in the projects and don't want anything more. We have those who are doing slightly better, but believe that the lottery, having their fortunes told, or staying on their jobs will bring them a miracle and improve their living situations. Then there are those who don't believe in waiting, become entrepreneurs, and do whatever is necessary to foster transformation and oneness with Good so that they can gain access to their "Promised Land" right here on earth.

They have no excuses. They will work and work to help free others along the way. This is the group that perseveres past struggle to success. Which one are you? Fear can inspire us to move forward or it can paralyze us and keep us stuck in the same place. It can also allow us to go only so far and then end up having to start all over again.

I was surprised when I learned that Harriet Tubman carried weapons while leading her passengers through the Underground Railroad. She used fear and the threat of violence to keep them moving forward. It has been documented that one of her passengers wanted to turn back because he was losing faith and was afraid of being caught.

She told him to either keep going or be killed. Harriet Tubman had never lost a passenger and she wasn't going to lose one. He decided to keep going and after just a few miles they made it to Canada. That story resonates with me because her conviction was so strong that she was willing to kill this man before she allowed his fear and lack of faith to interfere with her calling and purpose and the freedom of the other passengers she was responsible for. We have to have that same tenacity (without physically harming anyone) to allow nothing to sabotage our individual purposes, dreams, and quality of life.

Generational curses are real, and ignorance about our past as it relates to our future can no longer be an excuse. What you don't know can hurt you, and it probably already has. I am urging you to uncover the demons that exist in your lifeline. You cannot break invisible chains in your life without knowing where the chains came from, and, for that matter, what chains need to be broken, once and for all.

Identifying Potential Curses

By now, if you work in one of the helping professions, I hope you are viewing your clients differently. I hope that if you are trying to transform your life, you are viewing your family differently. I hope that if you are reading this to help someone you care about, you are viewing their life differently.

Now that you have the information, let's put it all together. How do you know if there is a curse or a spirit of wrong habits and wrong thinking operating in your family lineage or genealogy? These spirits abide where they feel comfortable and familiar. I wanted to make the answer to that question as easy as possible, so I did some research on my own family.

After viewing my family history and seeing all the recurring problems there were, it was almost inevitable that I would learn about some family curses. If you can say yes to any of the following questions, then I believe there are some negative habits and mind sets at work in your family system.

1. Is there a history of women in your family (or you) being unable to have children or having multiple miscarriages, still births, or abortions?

2. Is there a history of family alienation and/or parents not raising their own children (absent parent, children in foster care or given up for adoption), or feuding?

3. Is there a history of financial struggle, little or no progress, lack, or bankruptcy?

4. Is there a history of mental illness, drug and alcohol dependency, depression, suicide, or instability?

5. Is there a history of wicked speech, envy, and jealousy of thy neighbor, or competition and comparing oneself with others?

6. Is there a history of poor physical health, diabetes, high blood pressure, cancer, being overweight, etc?

7. Is there a history of sexual promiscuity or perversion (adultery, fornication, incest, homosexuality, rape, child molestation)?

8. Is there a history of idol worship (astrology, hypnosis, reading of tarot cards, being affiliated with occult religions, excessive tattooing and branding)?

9. Is there a history of domestic violence, divorce, single parenting, incarceration, and homelessness?

Awareness Is Preparation

After you have taken some time to ask the hard questions, observe or reflect on your life and are begin to see and study your personal genealogy, you may notice that you are not alone in your feelings, thoughts, and responses to life. You may even find that you feel angry because you wish someone would have shared and mentored you on these issues a long time ago. This is normal; it just means that you are enlightened and now have the working foundation to be the positive force in your family to rewrite the script of your family's future.

You are the agent through which change will come. You are the bridge that many will cross over into blissful living. The task of reclaiming and redefining your life is a challenging and delicate one but the end result makes it worthwhile.

The overall summary for the lesson in this chapter is that sometimes you have to dig deep to find out why you keep getting stuck in life. You have to uncover the painful past and important details of the past so you can rectify and begin to breathe new life into the generational wrong thinking and being.

You get the opportunity to be the shero/hero and save others from themselves. Most of all, you have to know that your history is the story of your past, but it does not have to be the foretelling of your future. What does your genealogy tell you about why you are where you are today? What I can tell you is you can come out of hiding now because it's NOT YOUR FAULT! Get the courage and rewrite your story the way you want.

Step 4: Rewrite Your Story

Chapter 4 Expansion Exercise
What's Your Story?

1. Create your family gene-o-gram and analyze your family patterns as far back as you can.

A resource I recommend is http://www.wikihow.com/Make-a-Genogram.

2. List the common patterns and see how it has affected your life. Decide how you will change the pattern and write your plan down.

Pattern	Affect on your life	How will you change it?

3. Make a video of your story and then rewrite the script of your life from a love and empowered-based theme.

4. Send an invitation for a family gathering to have an open discussion about the unsavory characteristics and offer solutions.

5. Release your family and self from feeling less than with situations that sprung out of control.

6. Frame the poem Children Learn What They Live as a constant reminder to give yourself and the next generation a truly "better" life.

7. Decide how you will memorialize your story so that it is never forgotten but it doesn't cause any more pain.

Chapter 5
Detox Your Life

Soulfirmation:

"Deep Down I Know The Truth And Releasing It Makes Me Happy And Free"

Courage is the New Confidence

Often, we don't realize that our confidence is deflated because the people we surround ourselves with usually have the same issues we struggle with – the desire to feel significant and wanted. When we live with invisible chains it can become difficult to figure out what we have been settling for in our lifestyle, relationships and self-care. Sure, we may be working and have a decent job, but are we living the dream life? Does the life we are living feel blissful and abundant? Most often the answer is no and the answer is no because it's unfamiliar to us.

It's unfamiliar because we have just done enough to get by. It's unfamiliar to us because we keep feeling we are not enough and that blissful abundant lifestyle is only for those that we believe have had an easier life than we. There is a saying that you will only be as rich, fabulous or happy as your five closest friends. If that's true that means look around and see yourself and evaluate your friends. Who among them would you like to exchange lives with?

When you are surrounded by mediocrity, confidence can be very intimidating. When you want change, confidence can be very intimidating. When you want to expand your lifestyle, and attract the right partner, confidence can appear impossible. However, I want to share with you that a lack of confidence is not your problem; your problem is a lack of courage. Because when you walk in courage you will feel your confidence rising. Courage to me is the new confidence.

Detoxify Your Life

The first step to walk in courage is to detoxify your life. It's time to look around at all of the things, people and situations you have been tolerating. Toleration is anything that makes you feel unappreciated, unloved, stagnant, bogged down, indecisive, raggedy, unattractive, unheard, misplaced, dirty, cluttered and out of alignment. Tolerating things keeps you playing small, settling and unaware of how powerful you really are. Tolerations weigh down on your soul and make you feel unattractive, heavy and emotionally drained. Tolerations are the invisible vampires that keep you from having the courage to follow your dreams and desires.

Tolerations are like carrying 50 grocery bags of rotten eggs. Tolerations are heavy and toxic, leaving a stench of unsavory energy wreaking from your soul and affecting your aura. Your tolerations attract low energy and low vibrating people in your life. They reinforce your fear based programming. These things lead you to abusive relationships because people can sense your low vibrating presence and realize that you don't value yourself.

They know this because they subconsciously see themselves in you and they know how to take advantage of your weaknesses. This is why you get looked over for the promotion, you can't catch or keep the ideal lover, you stay frustrated with your life, people mistreat you and you can't trust anyone. You buy a new car and it breaks down the second week. You get the hot sexy date and find out that he or she is emotionally unstable. You lose your wallet or end up missing your most needed job interview. Horrible situations are attracted to tolerations in you and me.

You see tolerations suck up your belief in you and the belief that Good is supporting you. In about the third session with a private client, we dive right into courage building by doing one or more of these three things to eliminate the tolerations.

1. *Complete It*

There's unfinished business you have been putting off, such as losing weight, painting a wall in your house, updating your resume, writing a book, getting your hair or nails groomed, cleaning the house. Unfinished and untidy things create frustration and block your confidence because (excuse my French) it's too much shit you have not completed. Your degree program, your certification, your business plan you have lingering. Tolerations thrive off of quitting or incomplete matters.

In order to have a boost in your confidence you have to be able to increase your personal WINS! When you win you feel good and when you feel good you attract good and when good is attracted to you, you feel confident. Between your unfinished business and confidence is the courage to complete it.

2. *Resolve It*

You feel insignificant and challenged because you have lingering issues with people, situations or within yourself that are unresolved. These unresolved issues attract more of the same issues. For example, you have a new love interest you have been speaking to and all of a sudden, they start exhibiting behaviors that you find either offensive or that are a big turn-off. Instead of having a "Classy Conversation" with the person, you hide, fade away, and become distant and quiet.

When they question if everything is okay, you say yes when you know it's not the truth. You think if you just get rid of the person, fade away or walk on eggshells, your problems are over. Low and behold, the next new love interest does the exact same thing, with some variations. The reason for this is because you did not resolve the issue.

Unresolved issues don't go away; they circle back like a boomerang. They return to keep you thinking that you that you are worthless and remind you that everyone is going to treat you the same way. The difference between unresolved issues and your confidence is the courage to bring resolve.

3. *Get Rid of It*

You don't like what you see when you look around you. You don't like how your bank account looks. You don't like how certain people treat you. You don't like how your job bores the hell out of you. You don't like how you look in certain clothes or with a certain image. The things you don't like are stifling your creativity and the flow of the inner powerhouse that you are.

If anything is hanging around your environment not fortifying your being and making your feel good, it's time to get rid of it. Hoarding and making excuses to keep dead people and things around is a sign that your fear change and that you feel like your identity is intermingled with the stuff you don't want to get rid of.

The more crowded your environment is with the wrong emotional toxins and mental baggage the harder it will be for you to feel like an amazing person because what you want and what you have are not in alignment. That alone makes you feel less than, when all you need is a simple tweak to your life and environment. This is the time you may have to solicit outside help to get you organized and bring out the best in you and your personal space.

However, once again the difference between getting rid of the things that are no longer serving you, including a bad attitude and your lack of confidence, is the courage to evict them and send them to their new destination far away from you.

As you evaluate your life and your environment, what do you need to complete, resolve or get rid of? If you can answer that and put action behind it you will feel your confidence rising. Confidence is a feeling and Breaking Invisible Chains is all about learning to feel your best!

Toxic Thinking is the Enemy to Confidence

Like many of the physiological detoxification programs, there can be side effects. You are ridding your entire soul of the dependence on years of learned behaviors and beliefs that served you up until the present time. This can send others around you into shock. You might even be tempted to retreat back into your old patterns, due to disbelief that the detoxification is working.

You may feel alone and you may even become afraid of the continual blissful feeling that you will experience. In our thinking, we have been taught to embrace the concept that states, 'When good comes, bad is on the way', or 'Nothing good lasts forever'. These are crutches that we use to limp along in a life that is unfulfilled. Some more examples of negative concepts or beliefs are:

1. Whenever I take one step forward I end up taking 4 steps back.
2. Nothing like that ever happens for me.
3. I have to wait to finish my education before I can do that.
4. I am not smart enough for that.
5. I don't want to be rich, just comfortable.
6. As long as I can comfortably pay my bills and have a little left over, I am cool.

If you have been comfortable with those beliefs and used them as crutches, then let me break it to you... If you have the courage to be bold and empowered during the detoxification, you will have to discard walking with your emotional crutches.

I don't want anything polluting my image of myself and my ability to have what I want. I have found that confidence is something you do have to fight for. All day everyday there can be energy draining, life deflating situations that make you question your worth and ability to feel on top of the world. Take it from me, you can have your cake and eat it too but once again that takes Courage to BE!

There is a three-step process that I use as often as needed to detoxify my thinking:

Remove Confidence Killers

A few years ago, I decided that I no longer wanted to be stuck living my life based on the hurt of the past. I felt compelled to share my experiences with the world. I found the courage to deal with my issues by sharing my story. I believed that I could be more helpful to others if I was transparent and honest about what was ailing me.

When I was able to talk about the past freely, I found that the reason I used self-sabotage as a crutch is because I subconsciously adopted my mother's critical perception of my actions. My mother's belief of me played like a broken record in my head, and from that opinion, my life was shaped. My mother was best at highlighting and over-emphasizing what I did wrong while never giving me credit for doing anything right.

I can remember getting straight A's on my report card in school. However, when I got home and showed her my grades she would always say, "You don't get a reward for things you are supposed to do." I was fifteen years old, and I could no longer live with the insults and being the constant target of my mother's anger. I gathered up my daughter and left home.

Why detoxification is so important

I finally left my mother's house at 15 years old and wandered from place to place with my daughter until I landed at my maternal grandparents' house. My younger brother was already there because he too detested my mother's violent outbursts. Plus, she could handle him no more than he could handle her.

When I got to my grandparents', everything seemed okay at first, but then it started. All the rumors I had heard about my grandfather were true. My brother shared with me how my grandfather, Pappi, had tied him up with a cable cord and beat him really badly to make him understand that he was the boss and didn't want any problems out of him. It hurt my heart because I didn't understand how my brother could go through so much physical and mental torment and not cry.

I remember one time when we were on our way to church with my great aunt and cousins in the car. My brother made my mom angry and before I knew it, she had taken off her shoe and was hitting him so hard on his head with its heel that she cracked his skull. To this day, the heel print remains at the top of his head and my mother denies that it ever occurred.

Seeking refuge at my grandparents', I had jumped out of the pot into the frying pan, leaving my mother to encounter the very person from whom she learned her ways. My grandfather was physically intimidating and was always so unpredictable. In addition, he and my grandmother would argue and fight day after day.

My brothers and I still laugh to this day whenever we remember how a Sunday school lesson between the two of them turned into a shouting and cussing match. How do you go from having a Godly discussion to hurling around insults in such a cruel and vile manner? It got to the point where I began to get nervous whenever I was in the house. One time, Pappi chased me around the house because he was in one of his fighting moods.

I swore to myself that I would kill him the next time he tried to hurt me. This the last time but having seen a blank gaze in his eyes, I knew that everything I had heard about him was true. I knew I couldn't stay there because anything could happen during an episode when my grandfather could not control his impulse to fight.

Pappi never acknowledged any wrong doing; he always acted as if he had done nothing. While being physically and verbally abusive, he maintained his position as a reverend in the church; preaching the gospel on Sunday morning but cussing and fussing Sunday afternoon clear to the next Sunday when it was time to return to church. My mother was a psalmist in the church, doing concerts and helping people feel empowered, but at home she was far from that.

Those are the people who initially shaped my view of God and of life. As you have already probably figured, I was scared of God and did not trust this place called life. Living in distrust kills confidence because confidence is a sign that you trust yourself, you trust the universe and you are sure that your life matters. Until you can know those these three things your courage will be stagnant and your confidence will be small.

That is why I am so thrilled to share my experiences with you because as you grow in courage you get your confidence back no matter what you've been through or seen. I am not the only one who was confused or traumatized as a result of my upbringing. But courage is doing what you have to using invisible forces until your feelings change and you master it.

You remember Rob… As soon as I turned eighteen, during the last year of my studies, I moved in with my high school sweetheart Robert (R.I.P. 1972-2003). I was struggling to find a place where I could feel safe and wanted. Prior to living together, we were best friends. We shared horror stories about growing up with domestic violence. We compared dysfunctional stories. We shared our dreams with one another, but most of all, we felt complete when we simply shared each other's company. Therefore, when he gave me a key to his apartment, I didn't hesitate to move right on in.

My boyfriend was everything to me until I began to talk about moving away to attend college. Then it happened. I was a little slave girl again, being bossed around, beaten, and threatened for wanting something more than living on a plantation. That's right. My lover boy turned out to be just like the other masters. He was controlling, jealous, and always smoking marijuana because he couldn't handle life. I even had to check in with him to get permission to run errands, and he would always accuse me of having an affair with my baby's father.

Then he would fight me and say demeaning things to me like, "I do it because I love you and I don't want to lose you. You're my star waiting to shine, but I'm not ready for you to shine just yet. But when you do shine, I want to be there with you." After the talks, he would offer me marijuana, and I would smoke along with him until I fell asleep.

I was so unhappy that it began to show in my physical appearance. I had become so unattractive, and instead of doing something about it, I totally let myself go. I gained a substantial amount of weight, and my hair started to fall out. This continued to happen until the day I learned that my freedom wasn't based on a physical place. It was a mindset. How did I learn this, after running from place to place, man to man, friend to friend, and state to state? I realized that there was one thing that never changed in all of these situations—me! I was with me everywhere I went. I was the common denominator. I knew that if something did not change, I was going to die. I finally decided to start cleansing myself from the confidence toxins.

Toxin removal meant I had to do something that I had never done before, be someone I had never been before, and ask for help in a way that I had never asked before. For me, the first step to my "Super Soul Detox Program" was to be totally honest about my feelings and then let it go. When I got it out of my system, it didn't hurt anymore. I had to allow the little girl in me to grow up.

I had to do away with just being seen; I had to be heard as well. I had to become selfish about my boundaries, my wishes, and my tolerations. I had to tell the truth, even when it hurt me and those who needed to hear it. It meant I had to walk alone many, many times. It meant I had to begin to honor the inner voice that lived in my gut not because I wanted to in most cases but because it was the difference between life and death and I finally chose to live!

I decided to stop being reckless with my life because it didn't edify the Good in me. It was only bringing shame because a bright pretty intelligent woman has no business allowing life to rob her of her purpose and her gifts to the world. When I decided to be a big girl about the very hurt sad me, a new method of crying clearly came to me - I began to write. My first book, I Fear No Evil for Thou Art with Me, was the beginning of my healing process. That is where I revealed how I really felt about my family and the trauma they brought to my life. As you can imagine, they were hurt, guilty, ashamed, and in denial.

However, it didn't make any difference because I had a right to empty out the trash that had kept me addicted to pain and misfortune and was fucking with my ability to feel good about me, my life and my future.

Understanding that removing toxins from my mind, body and spirit, has helped me become brave, bold, and fearless about freeing my children from the things that have almost demolished my own existence. I did not want to be guilty of understanding the invisible chains by not doing what I could to break the links that connected me to them. I did not have the wherewithal to do it just for me. I did it so that my children wouldn't relive my nightmare and to help you get your feel-good sassy back or for the first time.

Our relationships usually mirror situations or events that we experienced while growing up. That is why we say men marry their mothers and girls marry their fathers. We can only attract what is familiar to us. If those family situations or events were dysfunctional and abusive then we welcome the negative characteristics of others without realizing any damage being done.

This is the norm for us because we didn't have appropriate models or positive standards with which to compare right versus wrong and success versus failure. Even when family members realize that there is a destructive problem, either one of two outcomes occur: the situation is covered up and denied or there is an urge to overcome the odds and a fight for liberty begins.

Those who choose to cover up and deny the dysfunctional behavior or situation are the agents responsible for perpetuating the curse and the curse will only become stronger and continue forward toward the next link in the chain. However, those who are in search of truth and liberty usually become the sacrificial lambs who find themselves going through hell and high water. Only with much diligence, patience, and perseverance, they will prevail.

When we prevail at breaking the invisible chains, we get the opportunity to rewrite the script of our lives and the lives of the future generations that follow. The curse is stopped and soul harmony evolves. We then have the control to create a future of emotional happiness and joy that come with the abundance of peace and love. We are the future and it is time to make a change, even if it hurts. It is time for the "Super Soul Detox Program" because all those memories and feelings will stop us from getting to where we are going.

We must cleanse them and when we do, we must never let them back in again. There is now a new paradigm for us to live our lives by. *"We do what we have to until we can do what we want to!"* - Denzel Washington

Avoid the Pigpens

The associations you keep will reflect who you are at the core. I want to help you identify and eliminate the manifestations of your life, which I like to compare to the character Pigpen. Pigpen is part of the Charlie Brown Peanuts Gang.

Let's look at the personalities of each of the members and see how many of your friends and acquaintances match a character of the Peanuts Gang just for fun.

Write the name of your friend next to the character he or she resembles, but unless they have a great sense of humor, don't go and tell them they are the Snoopy or Charlie Brown of your life. Now let's take it a step further.

How many of these characteristics do you possess? Be honest. You can lie to me and your friends, but you cannot lie to yourself. That never works.

Character	Your Friend	Characteristics You Share
Snoopy — an extroverted beagle that daydreams on top of his doghouse and thinks he is a human being. He communicates through facial expressions but never says a word.		
Charlie Brown — something always goes wrong with situations in his life. He's a chronic worrier who frets over the simple things. Although he is concerned with the true meaning of life, his friends sometimes call him "blockhead." Charlie Brown has an obsession with putting himself down. But he finds a way to win in the midst of adversity.		
Woodstock — the smallest of the Peanuts characters, but has a big presence for a little bird. He can't fly, but he can type and take shorthand and is usually ready to do whatever the crowd is doing. Although he's the butt of many of Snoopy's practical jokes, he's his closest friend. Woodstock uses exclamation points (curse words) to express his emotions and temper.		
Linus Van Pelt — known for his "security blanket." He is the smart one of the group. He receives abuse from his big sister, Lucy, and Charlie Brown's little sister, Sally, is always trying to show him her love. However, he is not interested. While sucking his thumb, he is always putting life into perspective.		

Character	Your Friend	Characteristics You Share
Lucy Van Pelt — loud, bossy, crabby, and selfish. She's a know-it-all who gives her opinion and advice whether you want it or not. When it comes to compliments, Lucy only wants to receive them.		
Sally Brown — Charlie Brown's sister. She always looks for the easy way out. She tries hard to win Linus' heart and she has her big brother, Charlie Brown, at her beck and call. Sally, when not writing letters or doing homework, causes pain and joy in equal proportions.		
Schroeder — idolizes Beethoven. All he can do is play his piano, no matter what is going on. His piano playing is relative to everything.		
Peppermint Patty — great at baseball, but an all-around D student. Bold, brash, and tomboyish, what she lacks in common sense, she makes up for in sincerity		
Marcie — Peppermint Patty's best friend. Marcie has called Peppermint Patty "Sir" even though she knows she is a girl. They seem to have nothing in common, but that is what makes their friendship so great. Marcie is the smartest of the Peanuts gang, but also the most naive. If Marcie and Peppermint Patty ever have a falling, out it's likely to be over Charlie Brown, whom they both secretly love.		

Character	Your Friend	Characteristics You Share
Rerun Van Pelt — often mistaken for Linus, even though he's the little brother. He can always be recognized in his trademark overalls. Rerun also wishes he had a dog of his own, and because his parents won't let him have one, he borrows Snoopy. Snoopy is always rebelling against Rerun's obsession with him.		
Pigpen (our topic of discussion) — the butt of "dirt" gags. He walks around in a cloud of dust, getting dirt on everything with which he comes in contact. Pigpen is happily messy. He doesn't try to explain, hide, or fight it. For him, it's just a fact of life!		

These descriptions were taken from The Official Peanuts Web site: http://www.snoopy.com/comics/peanuts/info/reprint_info.html

How did you do? How many of your friends, including yourself, were a match with any of the Peanuts Gang? The point of this exercise is make you aware that the company we keep determines how far we can go. The revelation I got from the Pig Pen character was that although his friends and everyone who encountered him were agitated by his dirty dust, he never tried cleanliness. No one ever challenged him. I believe the friends he hung out with did not challenge him because they had their own clouds of dirty dust, as mentioned in the character descriptions. Confidence grows through overcoming challenges not staying the same and hanging out with folk who don't challenge us to grow. For every mountain you overcome your confidence rises.

What I have also found is that when we don't detoxify our souls, we will be drawn people who make us comfortable with being mediocre and assist our ability to attract drama and constant dilemma. We will draw people to us that don't remind us of our insecurities. Why? Because we view them the same way we view ourselves—people with a lot of issues. Have you ever had a relationship with someone who just drained you, yet you kept them around? Have you ever asked yourself why? We are comfortable with being comfortable.

The problem is that when you are comfortable, your dreams cannot be accomplished. Your dreams manifest when you are around dream catchers and your dreams manifest when you are actively taking risks to improve yourself and your environment. Dreams seldom come true hanging around the gang. You have been through too much to be ordinary. You have lived through too much to just get by. You have too much inside of you to just go through the mundane routine of existence. That is not what life is about. It is time to get the Courage to BE and live abundantly. But you must separate yourself from the Pig Pens in your life and you yourself must not be a Pig Pen.

I often speak with women about their relationships, and I am usually the first to point out that there is indeed a cloud of dirt dust following them. When healthy acquaintances realize that we have dirt dust following us, they don't want to be around us because we bring drama, confusion, and needless baggage. We bring them down. When our unhealthy acquaintances realize that we have dirt dust following us, they want to be around us even more because inwardly we desire their friendship and acceptance.

They are too happy to give it because it feeds their ego and somewhere deep down they are just like us. These are the friends who join our pity party and make our inappropriate behavior okay. As the old saying goes, "Birds of a feather flock together." What birds are you flocking with you? Is it time to depart flocking with birds because your confidence is calling you to soar with eagles?

Now What's Running Your Life

I couldn't get free for a long time because I had a fear of hurting my family and causing them embarrassment. My family was well known in my community. I knew that if I had exposed some of the stuff that crippled me I would be rejected and made an outcast. Later, I found out that people knew more about my family than I did. However, my past fear of causing discord and distress had already started to cause emotional and spiritual paralysis. Simply stated, I hadn't yet grown up. Emotionally, I remained immature. I responded to life's situations from the perspective of a twelve-year-old girl.

One day I was watching the self-help guru Iyanla Vanzant on the former reality television series titled "Starting Over." There was one woman who could not be genuine and could not be real because she was busy hiding behind a façade and blaming her absent father for her pain. When Iyanla got finished reading through her words and gestures, the woman realized it wasn't her father who was the culprit. She had been taught by her mother to view her father in a negative light and associate him with many of her bad traits.

Iyanla confronted her with the truth, which resonated with me. She asked the woman, "Who are you protecting by telling yourself this lie?" She asked the same question over and over until the woman broke down and started to cry, revealing that it was her mother whom she was protecting. From what I can remember, Iyanla said something like, "Who are you to lose yourself and your self-worth trying to protect people who need to hear and know the truth?"

That hit me like a ton of bricks. Who am I protecting by trying to keep the peace in the family? Who am I protecting while feeling down about myself every day? Who am I protecting while my life is so jacked up, while I hear the words of negativity being played in my head, causing me to gravitate toward people who reinforce the self-hatred that I've been struggling with since childhood? We are good at protecting others but now it is time to look out for number one. In order for me to thrive I must take care of my mind, my body, and my emotions. When I am detoxified from my past I can take care of myself in a healthy way.

I was able to identify some areas that subconsciously caused me to sabotage my progress because I used to repress the familiar feelings that I would get from my experiences growing up. If a situation reminded me of something from the past, I would deny it. For example, if I did not like how you spoke to me, I would leave and never return. That meant walking off jobs and ending relationships abruptly.

If I felt that you did not care for me, I would work that much harder to obtain your approval. I would do whatever it took because I didn't want any enemies. This caused me to reject anything positive. When something great happened in my life, I would say, "Let me enjoy it while it lasts." It was hard for me to confront the issues.

Since releasing myself from those negative patterns and holding myself accountable for having the life I desire and deserve, I have learned that I cannot live my life based on the fear of not being liked or not having enough. I now live my life based on the fact that there is much more than enough. I just have to be in the right space and the right place to experience it. Furthermore, I really do like me, and I don't worry about whether anyone else does or not.

Rules for Confidence:

These are the rules I live by, and since I have been doing this, I am truly a new creation. Confidence is my middle name.

1. Communicate feelings in a way that gives the offender a choice in how to deal with you. Always assume they didn't know what they were doing or how you would perceive their actions. Under no circumstances should you let your feelings stay bottled inside.

2. Understand that the issue must be resolved or your subconscious mind will keep creating the same situation because it is programmed to do so.

3. Don't run when you feel intimidated and uncomfortable. This is the ticket to further your growth and increase your maturity.

4. If you are involved in a relationship that just doesn't feel right, this is a spiritual indicator that there is a misalignment of beliefs, desires or characteristics. Do not try to figure it out, just know that when something is off ...it truly is. NEVER ignore your spirit guide. Often, we will lose our confidence because we didn't trust our spirit and that non-trust will lead us down the path to something destructive to the soul.

5. Don't make any decisions if you are not totally clear and at ease. That is a sign that you are being needy and fear driven.

6. Wait for confirmation; if it is for you, it will be confirmed at least two to three times.

7. Don't compare one relationship to another. This creates an automatic exit door. No two people are alike, but if you are attracting the same characteristics, you need soul detoxification before you begin a new relationship. Something in your soul is tied to the past.

8. Stop being a robot. The more you stick to the same routine, the greater the likelihood that you'll keep getting the same results. You should welcome growth and change. When you hinder your growth, you limit your ability to achieve wealth and happiness.

When you limit yourself, you limit your confidence.

9. Stop sharing the negative aspects of your life. Be careful what you say because life and death are in the power of the tongue. Speak to the positive and speak as though what you want is already happening. After a while, your mind will manifest what you are speaking. You don't want to be perceived as a negative person when you are a good person and have a lot to offer. Stay positive all the time no matter what. It will change your atmosphere and how you feel about you.

If you can follow these rules, you will see changes in your associations, income, and happiness. When I stopped letting people treat me any way they wanted and my aura demanded respect, I could feel good and confidence rising. It felt like the universe was giving me a standing ovation while I was graduating to being a full fledge goddess exuding power, living in wisdom and owning her personal power.

Of course, there were repercussions. I lost a great deal of people that I called friends but I gained the respect and admiration of the few who, like me, had the Courage to BE and held the ticket to the land of continuous blissful living! A land of soulful love that feels good. A place in my soul that I refer to as an unlimited supply of confidence.

This chapter is based on a simple question: Do you have the Courage to BE? The courage to be bold and empowered? The courage to be happy and whole? The courage to start all over if that is what it takes? Do you have the courage to evict everything and everyone from your life who is not enhancing your well-being? Breaking Invisible Chains requires a commitment—a commitment to your total being and acceptance of the fact that you are worthy of a life free of disease, fear, poverty, complacency, violence, and emotional instability.

A few years ago, some of my business partners and I created a Women's Empowerment Conference titled The Courage to Be. At this mini-conference, we saw hundreds of women thirsty and hungry for direction and makeovers from the inside out. We heard testimonies from women who were sick and tired of being where they were in life. We heard from women who were going through nasty divorces and were struggling single parents.

We witnessed women yearning to be a part of our happy inner circle of prosperity and wholeness. It became clear to me during the conference that women are tired of wearing the mask and carrying the loads of other people. They were sick and tired of life bullying them and sick and tired of not having the energy, time, or focus to live satisfying lives. It was disturbing to see so much agony, depression, and hopelessness, even in women who owned their own companies and were top executives in corporate America. Although they looked the part, their lives were out of control and they could not grasp the idea that soul harmony or peace could truly exist permanently in their lives.

Like children, they looked to us for the answers and we served as tour guides to a world of unity, sisterhood, and prosperity. However, the real answers to their deepest situations and concerns really came from their own souls. They just had to make up their minds to detoxify their souls and start anew. I will never forget a woman coming up to me immediately after the conference, sobbing, repeating, "I need y'all!" She wanted to learn how to be powerful within herself.

How often in your life do you feel like you are suffocating and can't quite put your finger on why you feel the way you do? You can't figure out why you can't get any further than where you are. It is because you have not been telling yourself the truth and you have been living with too much hurt and resentment. The greatest thief of happiness and joy is regurgitating the lies and secrets of the past, those energy killers and character assassinators from the past.

In summary, I want you to know that with the courage to be, you can rid yourself of the people or things that hinder you from being where you were created to be. But it is up to you to be competent and committed to doing what it takes to get yourself together. The difference between where you are and sparkling with confidence is having the courage to BE!

Step 5: Detox Your Life

Chapter 5 Expansion Exercise
Time to Detox!

1. List your tolerations and decide if you need to:

A. Complete it

B. Resolve it

C. Get rid of it

As you decide what needs to be done then create a time frame to get it done. This means make it a goal to get it done as quickly as possible. As you complete, resolve and get rid of your tolerations take notice to how your feelings about you and your life are shifting. Is your confidence muscle getting stronger? Are you smiling from the inside a lot more?

Toleration	Complete it	Resolve it	Get Rid of it

2. Who are the Pigpens in your life? Most importantly what about you is giving off the wrong impression and makes good quality opportunities and relationships repel you?

____

____

____

____

3. Who and what has been driving your life? What have been the confidence killers and are you ready to confront them or it? What is your plan to confront the confidence killer?

____

____

____

____

4. What 3 things will you do to step up your courage within the next 30 days? How will you celebrate when you have done it?

____

____

____

____

____

5. Identify your values so that you will understand when your boundaries have been violated. When you know what's valuable to you …it's hard to allow anyone to steal your good.

____

____

____

____

6. What other rules can you add to the list that boost and protects your confidence?

____

____

____

____

7. How do you feel when you feel confident? How can you feel that on regular bases?

____

____

____

____

____

Chapter 6
Feel Your Power

Soulfirmation:

"Actually, I can, I will, I have everything I need to be all that I need to be. The power is within me and I shall set it free."

Good showed me that the Boogie Man did not want me to progress, be healthy, and be whole. He wanted me to remember my ugly childhood and remain bitter. It benefited him if I always had strong negative emotions in response to the memories of my childhood. Now I understand that it is all about perception. My childhood was not all bad; it's just that the bad stuff was more memorable than the good because it left emotional scars. Now I magnify and memorialize the good things about my childhood. In the past, I was so busy nursing my pain that I was unaware of the angels that Good sent my way.

All of my experiences, good and bad, have played a major role in helping me express my talents and purpose of today. When I look over my life, I think about the character Dorothy in the motion picture The Wiz, because I was always closing my eyes and thinking of home. However, I really didn't know what it meant to go home or where home was since I was always running from place to place like a runaway. How would I know if or when I truly found it?

I learned from experience that home is in my heart and not in a physical place. It is a space and time in my life that was shared, influenced, and inspired by people who were critical to my growth, who blossomed and nurtured my gifts, and made me feel good and like I mattered. It seems like your greatest teachers and masters are only with you for a moment in time, but that is because they are filling your soul with their legacy. Once you have received their legacy, it's time to fulfill it.

Currently, home for me is Lagos, Nigeria. From the moment, I stepped foot in Nigeria, I was reminded of the bliss I felt whenever I spent time with my great-grandparents, Nana and Granddaddy. Granddaddy was a Baptist pastor and Nana was his stunning, highly-sought-after first lady. She really was the one who ran the church. Together she and Granddaddy shaped the first eleven years of my life. When Nana and Granddaddy were here, they taught me how to love. I believe I could recognize that same unconditional love through my husband. They continue to live on through my relationship with him.

They were my cheerleaders and I give them credit for my boldness and oratory skills. Nana taught me to read with emphasis and emotion at six. I was reciting poetry for the Christmas and Easter pageants by the time I was eight. I read the morning announcements in front of a huge congregation at nine and was a "Guild Girl" at eleven, two years younger than the required age. I was also the youngest president of the youth usher board and got my first job at McDonald's at the age of twelve.

Nana had already introduced me to entrepreneurship at the age of eight when she and Granddaddy hired my brother and me to clean their house every Saturday, so working at McDonald's at 12 years old didn't faze me at all. From these experiences, I learned to not let age keep me from doing what I wanted to do, and to press on until I achieved my goals.

Granddaddy was released from earth three years after Nana. When he died, I became aware of my spiritual gifts. The night he passed away I woke up like an alarm had gone off. Somehow, I knew that he had gone on to be with Nana. After they passed, I didn't understand why Nana and Granddaddy were taken from me but now I know that they weren't mine; they were loaned to me for a specific purpose. When they fulfilled that purpose, they were released to go to their heavenly mansion to receive the rewards they had earned by working long and hard on earth.

I can still remember being in the kitchen with Nana while she prepared supper and hummed the hymn Blessed Assurance. Even now, the words are so sacred and dear to me and I find myself humming the tune in my kitchen the same way Nana did:

Blessed assurance, Jesus is mine! O what a foretaste of glory divine! Heir of salvation, purchase of God, born of His Spirit, washed in His blood. This is my story, this is my song, praising my Savior all the day long; This is my story, this is my song, praising my Savior all the day long.

Perfect submission, perfect delight, visions of rapture now burst on my sight; angels descending, bring from above echoes of mercy, whispers of love. This is my story, this is my song, praising my Savior all the day long; This is my story, this is my song, praising my Savior all the day long.

Perfect submission, all is at rest, I in my Savior am happy and blest; watching and waiting, looking above, filled with his goodness, lost in His love. This is my story, this is my song, praising my Savior all the day long; This is my story, this is my song, praising my Savior all the day long. "Blessed Assurance" by Fanny J. Crosby, 1873

Fuel for The Spirit

Our greatest influences deposit something in us that nothing can take away, even if they don't always stay with us forever. That fuel is confidence. The confidence that if we use what they imparted in us, we will be okay. People go out of our lives for whatever reason. It can be very uncomfortable because the space we were holding for them is now empty. This becomes the place where our spiritual growth is fueled because the essence of Good is being demonstrated. Like Dorothy in The Wiz, my spirit grew stronger when I began to allow the greatest influences of my life to continue to live through me, although they were no longer with me.

With all the bitterness behind me, I now look through new lenses each day and know that Good is with me. Good is in me and because of this I can radiate joy. Every deposit from every significant experience in my life fuels my spirit and my joy. I thank Good daily that I am allowed to experience it.

In September of 2002, I lost my paternal grandmother who was also the matriarch of the family, Mama Maggie. Mama Maggie seemed so mean when I was growing up. She was five feet nothing and was a harsh disciplinarian with a voice like a man. But she was the one who instilled my manners, my quest for the meaning of life, and my need to research and analyze everything. She was the one who taught me to be open, honest, creative and spiritual.

Becoming gentler with her advancing age, Mama Maggie would sit down and tell me stories about the family and give me those womanly talks about the right and wrong ways to treat a man. She was the one who taught me how to spread a little and make it a whole lot. And she was the one who urged me to go as far as I could in school because she only got as far as the eighth grade.

She would talk to me for hours about life and living it. Mama Maggie was my cheerleader, too, especially when I moved to Cleveland to head a foster agency. She was so proud to see me go as far in life as I did. She held on to her faith that Good would find me a good husband and I would have more children. But I had simply been planning for her to come live with me. I was not ready for this, but I had to remember that our greatest influences don't stay with us for long.

Five years before her death, she was organizing her funeral. I did not want to accept the signs that she knew her time was really coming. Although I knew her health was failing, I still tried to make myself believe that she would always be with me. I was living in Cleveland, Ohio at the time and she was living in Columbus, which was about a two-and-a-half-hour drive away.

Whenever Mama Maggie would miss me or get depressed, she would check herself into the hospital and call me. The last time she checked herself into the hospital she didn't contact me. I had been calling her house for a week (she didn't have an answering machine) until the Holy Spirit told me to call Grant Hospital in Columbus, Ohio. The nurse in charge at the hospital told me Mama Maggie was there and was doing okay, but would not be released until the end of the week. She had renal failure and needed dialysis treatment. Right away, I remembered her always saying that she would rather die than seek renal treatment. The nurse asked me if I wanted to speak with her and I said I would call back the following day because I was upset that she was at the hospital and did not tell me.

The next afternoon I got a call from the hospital that Mama Maggie's heart was failing and that they had already revived her twice. I needed to get there right away because they needed me to make the decision on whether she lived or died. My heart was aching and I was scared. I couldn't believe that the little lady was really trying to leave me. I drove like a mad person all the way to Columbus. When I got to her hospital floor, my mother met me there. Both my mother and the nurse informed me of my grandmother's condition. They needed to see the power-of- attorney paperwork to determine that I had the right to make this important decision. We soon found out that I oversaw her finances but could not give orders not to resuscitate.

The medical care staff called my father since he was next of kin. Although at that point he had ignored her for several years, I believed he would make the right decision and come see about his mother. Well, he told the medical professionals that his daughter was in charge and to leave him alone. He didn't want anything to do with the situation and he slammed the phone down.

I know that my grandmother knew what was going on even though she was unconscious, because when I turned to look at her, a tear was rolling down from her right eye. I had never seen that much hatred in my life, nor did I understand why Good was allowing all of this to happen. I could clearly see that my grandmother's heart was broken and that she was ready to leave.

The hospital chaplain held me in her arms and told me to tell my grandmother that if she was ready to go, I would release her and allow her to be free. I thought that was the stupidest thing I had ever heard because I did not want my grandmother to leave me. But I had to be obedient because I knew deep down that she was confused about whether to stay or go, due to my father not giving them permission to allow her to live or die. She had to do it on her own.

I turned around to look at Mama Maggie, kissed her, and wiped the tears from her eyes. I told her that I appreciated her being in my life and sharing hers with me. I thanked her for guiding me into womanhood. I promised her that I would be the woman she had prayed for me to be and that I would not disappoint her or Good. I told her that if she really wanted to be with Good eternally, I was okay with it. Even though it hurt, I told her she was free to go, not to worry, and that I would take care of everything. Not more than two minutes after I said that, she transitioned to her eternal resting place.

The doctors came rushing in to revive her, but as they worked on her I saw a vision. I saw a huge angel sweep her up in his arms as if she was a little baby. They disappeared through the ceiling of the room. I began to pray in my heavenly language and joy filled my heart because I knew she was happy, and oddly enough, I was happy, too. At that moment, I was set free from the fear of abandonment. The doctors continued to work on her body, but she was no longer there. It was like her body had turned into rubber, and the soul I knew as Mama Maggie had ascended. She was pronounced dead just ten minutes later.

My grandmother's death didn't leave me feeling empty. It left me with a greater feeling of purpose and significance. For the first time, I could feel my power. She left me with the responsibility to break invisible chains that were keeping our family in a holding pattern of bitterness and pain. Her existence kindled the fire of the budding Ready Woman. I only wish she could meet my husband and my second daughter.

Death is not final and there is nothing to fear if you are a product of Good. Furthermore, the death of a loved one should be a happy time because that individual has fulfilled their purpose and we still should fulfill ours. Are you dealing with the loss of or separation from a loved one in a negative way? The Ready Woman accepts everything as it is and uses her power to create a message from what looks like a big embarrassing or hurtful mess.

The bridge to emotional growth and feeling powerful is shifting your perspective and gravitating with grit to the good, not the bad or the pain. Find a way to allow good in even if you feel betrayed and abandoned. Those are only feelings that reiterate your fears of rejection and worthlessness. A disciplined mind and heart finds the resolve in everything. She finds a reason to be happy. She finds a reason to trust. She finds a reason to feel powerful. Take the lessons and the love you shared and use it to fuel your confidence. You are one with them, and they are, and will forever be, one with you. Because they fueled your growth and fostered the journey toward being The Ready Woman!

"But those who hope in the Lord will renew their strength. They will soar on wings like eagles; they will run and not grow weary, they will walk and not be faint." Isaiah 40:31 (NIV)

Step 6: Feel Your Power

Chapter 6 Expansion Exercise Ready Woman Legacy Scroll

Create your Ready Woman Legacy Scroll by placing the names on the scroll of all those deceased and living who have strongly impacted the Good in you. Beside their names share the lessons of love that you will use to fuel your confidence when you feel a little lacking. When you've completed it, post it in a place that you can refer to when your confidence seems to be low and you are questioning your worth and value.

Look at your Sacred Legacy Scroll and say thank you to all the people that believed in you and wanted you to be successful so the power of their essence can live through you. If you like, you can use a Hawaiian Cleansing and Confidence Prayer that I often recite. Just had a bad and hurtful break up ...recite this prayer 3x a day. It will soothe your soul and enlarge your feelings of worth. Can you feel the power of The Ready Woman?

"Thank you, I love you, I'm sorry, please forgive me,
help me, show me the next best step!"

The Ready Woman
Legacy Scroll

Chapter 7
Unleash Her

Soulfirmation:

"No Limits, No Boundaries & No Regrets"

There are no quick fixes to becoming emotionally aware and mentally confident. However, there are methods I used consistently over time to transform the way I perceived my world and the way I manifested what I wanted. The ability to ask, own and manifest my soul's desires makes me a power-filled being.

I want to share with you how you can ask, own and manifest the life you've always imagined! The old way of operating from the left side of our soul dictated how we felt and what we could experience, such as depression, rejection, fear, suicide, and self-destructive patterns.

The right side of our soul gives us the power to create a new theme to govern our lives. It gives our soul the power to rewrite our script and manifest a life we can truly love. Soul Work helps us outgrow the familiarity of vibrating at the lower level of our existence. Now it's time to soar with ease because we have outgrown who we used to be.

The Power of Deliberate Creation

Now that you can create the life you want and love it, it is up to you to use your soul power to first ask for what you want through the power of deliberate creation. Deliberate creation is focusing on creating the life you want. Repeat these words: "I have the power of deliberate creation."

I want to take your life from good to great and from woe to wow. Personally, I was accustomed to a life that had more downs than ups. For every up, I had a series of downs. Because my programming was not set-up to handle longstanding success and happiness, my subconscious mind told me that I was not worthy of having everything I wanted. I would just settle and get a few things that I wanted.

As demonstrated in the graphic below, most people that I work with alternate between the lower levels of boredom, anger and/or depression. They toggle between being bored, angry and depressed with episodes of happiness. However, every day we should aspire to live between being happy and blissful. Living at the levels of happiness and bliss means we fill the wells of our soul by fully nurturing our presence and our physical, spiritual, emotional and mental selves. One of my first transformational lessons to prepare to become a wife was inspired from the scripture,

"But seek first his kingdom and his righteousness, and all these things will be given to you as well". Mathew 6:33 (NIV)

I say this because in the kingdom is power, authority and bliss. Therefore, for the first time I realize I wasn't seeking a place, I was seeking a feeling of power, a feeling of authority a feeling that all is and will be well. I was seeking the feeling and knowing that Good has my back. Seeking Bliss became this abundant feeling that I could have, do and be what I want.

The Challenge

Unless you work and become intentional about achieving bliss, it is not easily attainable and it makes the struggle to be happy, confident and clear toward achieving our goals difficult. It's difficult because it is related to the health condition of your soul. If your soul is filled with sorrow, pain and shortcomings, toxic beliefs or lack of love. You will be ruled by people and circumstances to keep you feeling these things. Having a blissful soul attracts its likeness, like soul mates, great careers, clients for your business and major opportunities you didn't work or ask for.

Your first job as *Matthew 6:33* urges is to seek bliss first. Then everything else is added and in the diagram, you will see how to step by step fill the wells of your soul.

To make it even clearer I make Bliss into a simple acronym to help me focus on the essential elements to keep my bliss FULL.

B - Beauty, how do I feel when I look in the mirror, how do I feel about my confidence, esteem and worth? Is my inside game free of difficult issues? Is my image or presence captivating?

L - Love, am I noticing the love all around me, am I receiving love from others with ease or am I rejecting and being critical, mean and ungrateful. Am I giving love to myself before giving to others? Am I kind to those I care about despite how they receive my gestures of love? Do I have clear boundaries and share my feelings and opinions in a loving well for the best interest of all involved.

I - Intuition, is my spirit guiding my decisions or am I overriding my spiritual knowledge with fear, popular culture, desperation or pressure from outside entities. Do I know the difference between my soul is crying and the spirit speaking, giving me signs, clues, and nudges? Is my yes, a sure yes and my no a sure no without regrets?

S - Sensuality, do I have the confidence to own my feminine essence and be proud that I am a woman and hold power to the heart of a man? Am I okay with my voluptuous breast, wide hips, soothing voice, a provocative stare that makes a man melt? Can I still feel gorgeous and flaunt without being intimidated by other women, fear I am being to forward and seeking trouble or the cause of a man's nature rising.

Can I be me with two stomachs and the scale reading me as being twice my standard size? When the time comes can I be the freak in the sheets without feeling like a whore or being judged?

S - Significant, am I that chick who is making an impact on her purpose and allowing Good to use me as a representative of His liking and namesake? Am I exemplifying the epitome of the Ready Woman who is turning her challenges and problems into a platform of income and influence? Is my spirit strong enough to keep my husband's attention while forming a legacy in the world? Am I making someone's life easier, happier and prosperous each waking day? Do I know who I am, who I belong to and am I proud of where I've been and where I am going? Are my light and life shining?

Filling the Wells of Your Soul to BLISS

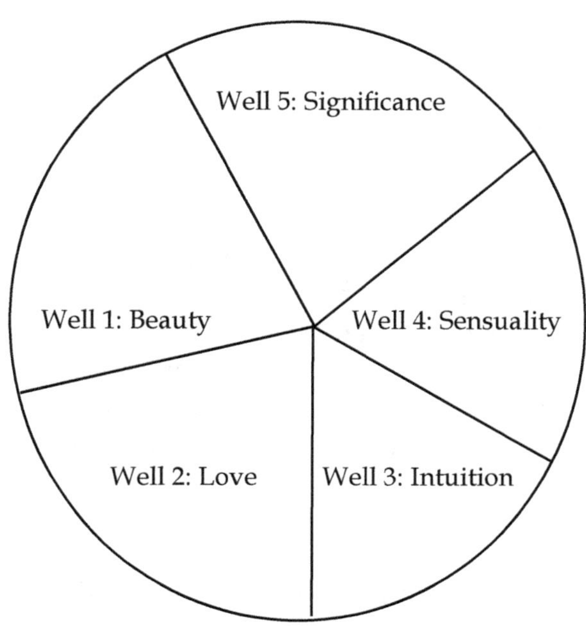

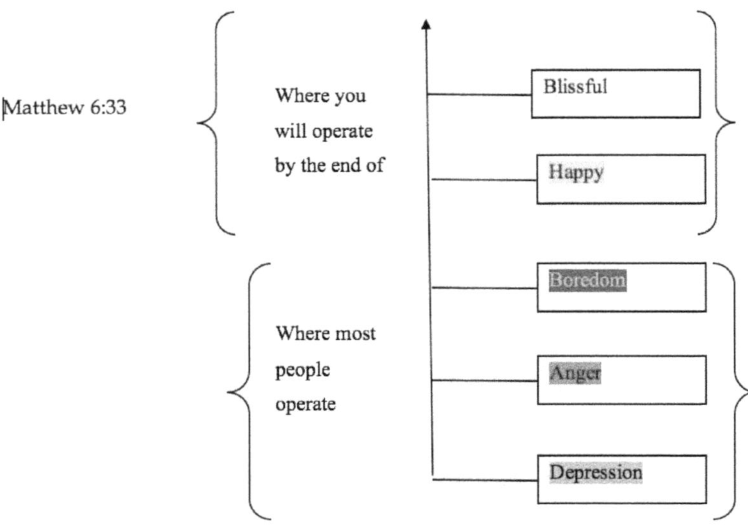

I used to believe that having only have a few wells of my soul filled was better than not having any. Then the light bulb turned on and I recognized that I was vibrating a low frequency after watching a hot DVD titled "The Secret." Viewing "The Secret" helped me understand that although I was healed from my past and it no longer brought me sorrow and pain, there is more to healing.

I learned that for someone to be happy and blissful, you have to fill those wells with who you want to be and imagine what you want in the well. In the end, what you want will take up residence in the wells of your soul before it manifests itself materially. Just like a child learns to sit up, crawl and then walk, so it is with creating a new theme for your life.

You should fill your mind and spirit with what it needs to create a life that will help you fulfill your soul purpose and manifest your soul desires. Deliberately creating your ideal life draws everything to you that you are supposed to have.

Focus on what you want so you can have more of that. Don't, for one second, add energy, emotion, or even talk about what you don't want. That was my issue all along. I was focused on avoiding things and what did I get? More of what I was avoiding or running from. Allow me share an instance of how subconsciously deliberately created the wrong situation which created so much drama.

3 Days in Jail Breaking Chains

I spent three whole days and two nights in jail. I was a grown woman, but I was handling my problems like a girl. A situation had occurred at my daughter's high school when she was 16. Ciera, who I had given birth to when I was a teen, had been jumped twice by some gang members in her school, simply because they did not like her. The school and the local police department were dragging their feet to bring justice to the matter. All along, I kept rehearsing over and over in my head that if they didn't get it together, I would.

Finally, the opportunity presented itself and that was the final straw for me. The school called and told me that my daughter was attacked. When I arrive at the school, with my newborn baby, I was furious. They escorted me to the conference room where my daughter was in the corner and there was a table of teenage girls in the same room. I saw my child with her clothes torn and her hair all over head. I spoke to Ciera and asked her what had happened. She told me that she was sitting in class doing an assignment and a gang of girls came into her room and attacked her. I asked her who did this and she pointed across the room to the table with the girls.

They stared back at me with a look that I interpreted to mean that were not afraid to fight me too. I asked Ciera to point out the group leader. After she identified the leader, I instructed my daughter to "get up and whoop her ass!" My daughter did what I told her do and started a fight with a leader. The other girls jumped in to protect their friend and Ciera did not back down.

I didn't think twice about what I was telling my daughter to do and didn't realize the implication of what I was saying. This was my old subconscious programming taking control of my decisions. As a result, I spent three days in jail, where I was treated like an animal with possible felony charges of inciting a riot.

Everything I previously imagined about jail had manifested. I had to sit and sleep on the floor and share food with prostitutes and drug addicts, all while wearing the same clothes the whole time. I had to use the bathroom in the same place where I laid my head and there was no privacy. There was no television or radio, and only one fifteen-minute phone calls a day. I was surrounded by stone walls and iron bars for seventy-two hours, thinking about what I had said and the outcome, while trying not to freak out over what was about to happen to me. My life was now in the hands of the judge and the police department felt I was worthy of a felony conviction for inciting a riot.

I had created a mess for myself, not to mention I was a breast-feeding mother of a four-month-old. My baby was without food, Ciera left to live with my relatives in another city until we moved four months later, and my husband was left with this mess to clean up. This is what my imagination and thoughts had manifested, and I had to suck it up.

I was in jail with other women who had manifested their situations as well. Our education, profession, where we lived or the type crime we allegedly committed was irrelevant. We were all in this place together. We were all offenders of the law and we were in a place designed to detain those who break them. All of us were living within the lower levels of our lives.

During my time in jail, which was the longest three days of my life, I could spiritually make sense of what was happening to me and I could see the commonality among all my cellmates. Most of us had undergone some sort of childhood trauma and we were all bitter and felt a sense of powerlessness. We were all vibrating below happiness and therefore, various circumstances in our lives reinforced the emotional trauma and deep worthless feelings about ourselves.

Each of us were mentally in jail long before we had physically arrived there. So, during my last night of being detained, I had a long talk with one of my cellmates about invisible chains. She revealed that she was a hairdresser who smoked and sold crack. Her rationale for her lifestyle was, "I'm mad at God for taking my kids' father from us and for taking my mother from me." She used the power of deliberate creation to magnetize anything that reinforced her grief and powerlessness.

So, did every other woman in there. We were grieving and feeling powerless over our situations and emotions. That powerlessness translated into invisible chains—the enemy we couldn't see with the natural eye but that controlled everything and came to kill, steal, and destroy our Good and authentic purpose. This behavior, pattern, way of feeling and living was depriving us and stealing from us BLISS.

Bliss is the power that breaks the invisible chains. From then on, I knew I did not want anything to have that much influence over my life that would keep me in a pattern of boredom, anger and depression. The Ready Woman that as emerging was for once truly empowered and raging with vigor from deep in my soul, "Unleash Her". Deep inside my soul while in jail the caterpillar had transformed into a beautiful and free butterfly. I knew that it was time to achieve Matthew 6:33 with tenacity because without BLISS I would be forever burdened with past emotional and mental programming of a life that didn't make me feel good or make me the best representation of Good!

Saying Yes to Bliss with the Story of Jonah

In my distress, I called to the Lord, and he answered me. From the depths of the grave I called for help, and you listened to my cry. – Jonah 2:2

My experience in jail reminded me of the biblical story of Jonah and the whale (Book of Jonah). Jonah was a Hebrew who God wanted minister in Nineveh, a place filled with immorality and wickedness. Jonah didn't want to obey God and he tried to do his own thing and go wherever he pleased. Because Jonah was disobedient, God caused a terrible storm while he was in a boat with other men, moving away from Nineveh. Jonah realized that his disobedience had caused the storm and asked the men to throw him overboard. At first, the men refused but the storm got worse.

Eventually they threw him in the sea and the waters became calm. While in the sea, John was swallowed by a whale where he lived for three days and three nights. During that time, Jonah began to pray and remember how good his God is and how it is better to do what God is calling him to do than to ignore it. After Jonah repented to God, the Lord commanded the fish, and it vomited Jonah onto dry land.

Like Jonah I realized the error of my ways, and after my 3 days in jail, my day in court came, and the judge asked me what I had learned and how I would do things differently if the situation presented itself again. I stood with a new sense of Good and happiness in my heart, and with sincerity; I shifted the story from blame and hurt to ownership and power by admitting I was wrong. I admitted that how I responded to the situation could have led to a far worse outcome than it already had.

I could have handled the crisis without displaying such strong emotion because I did not feel heard or safe. I could have more vigorously pursued legal action. Most of all, I could have listened to my intuition for enlightened guidance. That situation humbled me and helped me see that if I could manifest that type of toxic and volatile situation, then I was powerful enough to manifest my ideal life with the power of deliberate creation.

Right Soul Process to Create:

The powers of deliberate creation is key to manifesting the life you really want. You know from my challenges to not focus on or put energy behind what you don't want. Now that we have dealt with the Boogie Man, we understand our soul and how to revive our spirit. We've been challenged to tell a new story that is more in alignment with all things working together for Good. We've learned to release our tolerations and anything or anyone hindering us from a life that feels good. We have certainly regained the knowledge of how powerful we truly are. Now to ensure we have the tools needed to break invisible chains and fully embrace our new identity as a Ready Woman, we will end this chapter with learning how to consistently use the power of deliberate creation to create rituals that fuel our BLISS.

Beauty of Vision

It is so important to me that I begin my morning with meditating on and visualizing my goals and dreams. While doing this, I pray to God and thank God for all that it has allowed to come my way, including the things I don't understand.

I sit with my dream board in front of me. Now, some people have big dream boards, but mine is the size of a place mat and it is laminated. My board is not a representation of solely materialistic items and possessions I want to have. It contains the theme of my life- Heal, Love & Live Your Bliss. It is everything I desire, inside and outwardly, plus all that I want to feel, be and do.

I keep my board on my sacred altar, which for me is a space on my bookshelf in my office. There is a beautiful, warm feeling that comes over me as I am visualizing, and great expectation takes over. When I feel that, I go back to my "I AM!" and I remind myself and Good that I know who I AM! In addition to my visualization board, I have index cards that I carry with me on a ring with my goals and visions written down.

Throughout the day, I flip the cards to different aspects of my life and state aloud what they say. As a result, everything I ask for comes to me somehow, some way. I don't worry about how it will come; I just know it is coming. At nighttime, before I go to bed, I stare at my board and again, I begin thinking about how awesome it is to finally have a life that I love. Then I write down what I need to accomplish the next day. Jack Canfield stated in his book, Success Principles, that when you write it down the night before, your subconscious will begin creating opportunities to complete the task. Again, you are teaching your mind, will, and emotions the power of deliberate creation.

Be Led by Your Intuition

I no longer just hear with my ears. I hear with my spirit, my intuition. When you are a person of faith, you cannot always rely on what you see, but what you sense. You should trust the guidance from your intuition and understand that it is Good speaking to you. You should trust that inner voice that speaks, prepares, and warns is Good. What I have found is that some people have a need to use logic one hundred percent of the time or else they don't believe in it. That is why business deals crash and relationships don't work out. They thought through situations logically without paying attention to what they sensed.

There is an exercise I do now that I kind of made into a game. Before I make any decisions, I answer based on what I sense. It is what I am feeling in the pit of my stomach. Whenever I take the time to do that, I don't go wrong.

If you practice listening to what your gut is telling you, the more faithful you will become. So, the next time someone says, "I heard Spirit saying to me..." they are saying that the Good within them is speaking and they are smart enough to listen! The more you listen the stronger that voice becomes and you will manifest your desires with more ease because you are using supernatural flow vs. hard work.

Because I was raised a Christian, I call my inner voice of reason, safety, and guidance the Holy Spirit. In John 21:18, Jesus says: I tell you the truth, when you were younger you dressed yourself and went where you wanted; but when you are old you will stretch out your hands, and someone else will dress you and lead you where you do not want to go.

Acts 1:8 states: But you will receive power when the Holy Spirit comes on you; and you will be my witnesses in Jerusalem, and in all Judea and Samaria, and to the ends of the earth.
Allow me to share with you the following three true stories so you can understand how powerful it is to be in partnership with GOOD through the Holy Spirit, your divine guidance, intuition, YOUR RIGHT SOUL POWER!

The Residential Facility

I used to facilitate a women's rehab group and at the end of every session, I would gather the women in a circle and give each one of them a positive affirmation about herself. On one occasion, I heard Holy Spirit say, "Tell her if she goes back out there (meaning drugs and prostitution) that she will die." Of course, I felt terrible because this was the time when I was supposed to be affirming them.

I struggled for a few seconds and then told her the message I received for her. I saw the tears flowing from her eyes and she never said a word. A few years later, I was sitting in ministry school and a beautiful, petite African American woman approached me. She had such a radiant glow and a pleasant and smooth voice. She said,

"Is your name Nekisha?"

"Yes," I said.

"Do you remember me?"

"I am so sorry, but I don't."

"I'm Bernadette. I was in your women's group a few years back. You told me if I went back out there I would die." She went on to say that she had just about given up and was contemplating ways to AWOL or abandon the program without approval. Bernadette went on to say, when I shared what Good revealed to me, it felt like lightning had hit her entire being and she felt an instant shift in her belief and consciousness.

She felt an indescribable feeling of strength to win and heal. She said she made a declaration that she no longer needed the streets and from that day forward she had been clean, sober, and turned her life over to Good.

She was now an evangelist and traveled from place to place sharing the good news of how Good had set her free from the bondage of drugs. I began to weep. Up to that point, I wondered if my efforts to change lives were making a difference. This was my confirmation that right soul power was the best, purest and most satisfying place to live from.

The Upstairs Neighbor:

I had a neighbor who called me because she was feeling sad. She asked me to pray for her. I said yes and I began to pray. During the prayer, I heard the Holy Spirit say, "Tell her to drink three full glasses of water." I struggled with that because I didn't understand what drinking three glasses of water had to do with what I was prayer with her.

But I kept hearing it over and over: "Tell her to drink three full glasses of water." Feeling stupid and awkward, I stopped the prayer and said, "Donna, I need you to drink three glasses of water and make sure you do it when we get off this phone." Through heavy sobbing, she said okay. She didn't ask any questions, thank Goodness, because I didn't have any answers. The next afternoon she came over to my house to thank me for being attentive to her the night before. She told me that before she called me, she was craving alcohol and wanted to get drunk.

She had gone up to her neighbor's house to drink with her, but the neighbor needed fifteen minutes to get her house straight. In the meantime, Donna came downstairs and felt impelled to call me. When she drank the three glasses of water, she said the desire to drink the alcohol instantly left her and she had a restful night's sleep. Well, once again the Holy Spirit prevailed through me, and another life was saved from self-destruction.

Church Member's Job

It was prayer time at church and we were all gathered around the altar singing, holding hands, and praying between the singing. I felt the Holy Spirit tell me, "Touch the man beside you and tell him he got the job." I was not feeling that at all. I was in a new church and didn't know a soul. So, imagine how I felt hearing the Holy Spirit tell me to let some man know that he got the job. How crazy is that! Well, I took the risk and leaned in toward the man and said, "You have the job." The man looked at me with a straight face and said okay.

My heart had never pounded so fast. In fact, I tried to run out of there as soon as possible because I did not want to be embarrassed by saying something that was irrelevant to this man. Two weeks later, the same man approached me in church and said, "Sister Nekisha, I got the job!" He went on to say that he had secretly applied for a job at the post office, but he didn't tell anyone, not even his wife, because he did not want to be embarrassed or disappointed if he didn't get the job.

He said he wasn't even qualified for the job. But he was called in for the interview the day after I told him he had the job, and by the next week he was given an offer. His income was now bigger than it had ever been before. To Good be the Glory! In your right soul is direct communication to the mysteries and wisdom of the universe and to flow in that wisdom means The Ready Woman is UNLEASHED!

The Power of Praise

Focusing on gratitude and praise teaches us to appreciate where we are and the direction in which we are going. It demonstrates that we are not bitter or angry. Being grateful teaches us to look to the future with optimism and great faith that the years ahead will be a whole lot better than the ones we've already been through. Being grateful openly says to Good, "I don't understand everything, but I know day by day you are sculpting me to be a beautiful masterpiece worth more than money can buy, causing admirers to wonder how I got to be so beautiful and worth so much." The power of gratefulness comes through our ability to be mindful in praising Good because we have been chosen to represent live happy and with power. Gratitude is a GOOD magnifier and expansion of better and best.

Praise creates empowerment and reestablishes our focus and trust that somehow Good will make the path clear for us. Praise is a spiritual weapon that confuses the Boogie Man in our head. The Boogie Man wants us to be disgruntled and full of fear and resentment, but praise cancels all that out and commands Good to help us in our times of need, as well as thanksgiving for all that has already been done.

Isaiah 61:3b states: ...to bestow on them a crown of beauty instead of ashes, the oil of gladness instead of mourning, and a garment of praise instead of a spirit of despair... There is power through praise, and we were created to praise because praise accelerates your ability to manifest your desires. Just let praise be something you do unconditionally. Even during pain, remember to focus on praise. That is the secret weapon of acceleration.

Love Drama

Before going any further, I must cover the all-important area of love. To prepare myself for marriage long before I was dating again, I used to imagine myself being in a wonderful relationship with a wonderful, caring man. I even used to set a place for him at the dinner table and—don't laugh—I bought him a toothbrush. I started attending marriage seminars as a single person because I knew that my time was coming and I wanted to be married.

Because I had been with abusive men in the past, I didn't want to carry that into the future. I read and studied every book I could find about selecting the right person and what to do before saying 'I do.' I even learned how to cook two good meals: meatloaf and spaghetti.

I educated myself about diamond rings, and when there was a sale on wedding bands at a store downstairs from where I used to work, I laid one away and purchased it for my future husband. I know you think I'm crazy, but I was simply focusing and holding a space for what I wanted the most. I was preparing myself for my new arrival. I also began to study the stories of the marriages—good and bad—in the Bible, and what love is and is not.

I had to learn to express the love that goes beyond physical attraction and words. When I was chained, I thought love was just about sex, manipulation, control, and even violence. I thought it was based on looks and money. Now, as a Ready Woman, I understand that love is indeed about commitment to each other's wellbeing, creating opportunities for healing and growth, respect and legacy building. Love is about merging into a power couple, and power couples are not just monetarily rich but emotionally wealthy. Wealthy and blissful minds, intentions, purpose, and vision are what I was looking for in my next relationship as I prepared my body and mind for love.

In the introduction, I told you about my first husband. Can I tell you, I had to have him as a husband because he came to shake me up and show me what I did that caused my life to be out of order? I thought because I was a plus size girl, I would never find anyone to marry me. Secondly, I was celibate and when I would tell guys that, they would run like a thief and he didn't.

Although I was celibate and waiting on Mr. Right, I wasn't healed in my soul, and as you may know, I had not achieved BLISS. I only had the energy to gravitate toward lovers and people who reinforced how I felt about myself. He was a cobra, and so was I. He mirrored in the worse way how I felt about me. I acted like I had it all together and loved myself but I didn't. I didn't know love, and I thought it had to hurt or I had to work for it.

My father taught me to chase after men to get them to notice me. He showed me that through his disappearing acts in my childhood and even as an adult. Because I wanted a relationship with my father badly, I did just about everything to keep him in my life. That same sentiment is how I fostered my love relationships. But just like my father, they would never last. I would end up hurt. To the point I didn't believe in love nor did I think love was real.

After my divorce, I dated a guy and his family, I thought we were a cute couple, he was in the church, a worship leader to be exact. I remember asking him did he feel we were soul mates and he said no. But I like a challenge so I campaigned for his love, doing everything I could to make him and his family happy. After six months of thinking I had finally won him over, I went out of town on business.

While I was out of town, I noticed that our phone calls were becoming distant and less passionate. Finally, I asked him what was going on, and if I was nothing, he broke up with me and said a relationship with me would never work.

I was too old and too fat. I became obsessed, crying begging trying to talk things through. One day, he called me and said, we will never be together, and I will pray for you that you can move on. He did just that; he prayed for me on the phone that I could find peace and move on.

A Break in the Man-Cation

It was a terrible night for my soul, but these things happen until you unleash the Ready Woman fully. After a few months, I vowed to go on a man-cation. It's a vacation from men and relationships. During this time, I created a vision board in December 2011 for the year 2012. On my vision board, I had a trip to Africa, I would be self-employed, I would lose weight, I would learn to meditate and that I would be engaged to my soul mate.

A few months later, I met this "nice" guy who was a film and music video producer on social media. Twitter to be exact! He was attracted to my caramel skin, baby face and afro that was not manipulated by Photoshop. I was attracted to his chocolate skin, intelligence and that Harlem N.Y. accent. I remember the day we took our conversation from Twitter to the phone, I needed his help on a project and he made time for me. It was so serendipitous because he was what I thought I wanted at the time.

I wanted him, I could see a future with him, but I needed him to want me too. So, after our first phone call he texts me back in 15 minutes and said, "Yo, I didn't want to get off the phone with you." My fingers started texting before my mind could catch up. I text back, "OMG I didn't either, I thought it was just me." A few hours later we were on the phone talking for 4 hours until we both fell asleep.

After which, a few days passed I didn't hear from him, and I could feel that sad sinking feeling. That feeling that said you know this is too good to be true. No reasonable man wants you. You're also fat, and hot men don't like fat women.

Chasing My Prize

You know what some of us women do when the silence becomes so unbearable. We take control and chase what we thought was the ideal situation. Not knowing that when a man disappears, he's either trying to figure out if he wants to take it further or he's moving on to something else that has his attention.

After four days, I decided to text, and after the text, he texts back and on and on we texted and talked. I never took notice I was the one always doing the initiating, but looking back it was because I thought I found a good thing and wanted to do everything I could to please him so I could keep him.

After three months of talking and thinking I was in a long-distance relationship filled with days and weeks of silence that I thought was due to his long days on set and editing. I began calling psychics to see where our relationship stood and he finally decided to visit me in Los Angeles.

I planned a fantastic weekend of fun, food, and romance. It all went down, Kevin stayed at my place, and we had a long steamy hot weekend of fun, food, and love. The sex with Kevin was so good that I cried. We had fun until we fell asleep laughing. The food was excellent and we had the best conversations while indulging our taste buds. It all got messed up when Monday morning arrived.

We took a walk on the beach eating and sharing ice-cream, he was calling me babe and then I took him to the airport to catch his flight. We hugged, and he told me he had a great time. He texts me to let me know he made it back to Harlem NY and I never saw him again. He cut off all forms of communication with me.

I checked his social media accounts, to realize, he blocked my access. I called his phone, and it wouldn't go through. I text, and he would not return them. I emailed, and he remained silent. All I could think was, but he said he loved me. I realize much later in my journey that love doesn't mean devotion and often like doesn't even mean the same thing to two people who share chemistry. That is when I understood that chemistry does not indicate compatibility.

There I was again, feeling dejected, confused, unloved and ashamed. I knew for sure it was my weight that kept me from love. However, once again I got the strength to seek Good and ask for help in finding the truth about love. If it was real, I wanted it without any more abuse, heartache, and abandonment.

One More Chance at Love

When it hit me the man that I had fallen in love with was gone, and he left a big gaping oozing hole in my soul. There I was having a conversation with suicide and Good at the same time. To suicide, "life sucks, love is not real, and I don't know why I am here." Then to Good, I said, "is this all there is to life? Pain, failed relationships and working jobs you hate." This was in between the crying, fits of rage and hiding under my blanket in bed in the dark for days.

One Sunday, I came from underneath the blanket long enough to receive a fresh wave of inspiration and hope to watch Orpah's "Super Soul Sunday". I fell in love with the peaceful, optimistic teachings of internationally renowned Buddhist Monk, Thich Nhat Hanh and read his book "No Death, No Fear" that filled the aching part of my soul with such profound peace and sense of knowing that love didn't leave, but it had changed its form. In his book, he shares that nothing ever dies it just transforms into something else, and it is up to us to recognize the change and accept that nothing stays the same. For example, the ocean, the rain, the clouds and the water we drink. Never dies just moves to something useful and that we should redefine its meaning and listen carefully to its whispers.

It was at that moment I realized the Kevin, the guy that disappeared from my life didn't abandon me, he gave me a reason to give love another chance but this time not with a man but with myself. Taking time to explore deeply why did a relationship with him means so much to me and why was I crushed. The reason, I found deep inside is that I wanted to be a wife. I wanted to be happy, and I wanted to feel significant to another being because since the passing of Rob my first real love, my grandparents and most recently my father; I felt out of place, lost and alone.

The work became clear through countless hours of studying Thich Nhat Hanh's teachings and participating in his meditation retreats a Deer Park Monastery in Deer Park, California that I had to learn to create what I wanted to feel and be for myself and with myself. While studying spiritual guru Gary Zukav's book, "The Seat of the Soul" which taught me the power of managing my emotions and being intentional about what I wanted in life not from my needs being deficient but from the ability to create an abundance of love from within me. The wealth of love replaced the void Kevin left inside me, and in 6 months I attracted the love of my life.

Bliss is Full

For six months I was on a mission to fill my joy, and just as I created on my dream board, afforded the opportunity for my youngest daughter and me to travel to Nigeria, West Africa for December 2012. There I am sitting in the bedroom of my hostess home writing in my journal after being there for nearly two weeks. I never forget it was December 20 close to midnight.

I was sharing my gratitude to Good for allowing me to experience such a fantastic transformation and to have blessed me with 80% of the request I had on my vision board.

As I was thanking Good, I remember saying these six months have been fantastic, and I am an entrepreneur, I lost 50 lbs., my skin is radiant. I am a religious meditator, and I have met some tremendous men who enjoy my company. My income has increased, and now I am spending my vacation in Lagos, Nigeria. My soul filled with love and bliss. I said but Good, I still want to be a wife and whatever I need to do or become, please continue to show me, help me make the next best step. I closed my journal got into bed and allowed my peaceful sleep to overtake me.

It Happened

The very next day December 21, 2012, started off normal. I slept until I felt like waking up and I told my host to leave me behind, the host and my daughter were going out to get a Nigerian passport. The passport was for Islamyaat my youngest daughter, but I thought they would not need me. I wanted to soak up the sun and meditate because since being in Lagos it has been parties, visiting and being treated like a celebrity on tour and I was exhausted by all the love and attention directed toward me.

My meditation was interrupted by a bang at the door from one of the children in the compound estate where I was staying. He came to let me know that I should dress up and that my host was coming to pick me up because the passport office needed my signature.

I was not happy, but I made myself beautiful with my cute summer halter black dress with a neon pink tank top. My sparkly sandals on my feet, I pulled my hair into a ponytail and gave my self a natural makeup look. When they arrived, I was ready, and my spirit was very elevated. I put on my sunshades got my Blackberry and headed out the door to the car.

To my surprise, it was a different car with a male driver. That is when it happened, holy mother of Jesus. At that moment I am introduced to the most amazing, handsome 6'2 athletic shaped, spiritually balanced and smart man I have ever met.

The chemistry, the conversation and the identical life goals made us inseparable. In fact, it was divine fate and an unforeseen introduction that brought us together. Boyo, my husband and soulmate said to me he was not supposed to be in Lagos during the time we met. He was supposed to be on an extended business trip, but six hours away from Lagos he didn't have a settled spirit.

He said he had a deep urge nudging him to get back to Lagos. He was obedient to his intuition and he arrived back in Lagos December 20 and met his queen the next day. (Hallelujah).

I was in Nigeria to connect with my roots and elevate my bliss, but that trip gave me so much more. I learned my interpretation of Matthew 6:33 is correct. All the work to fill my BLISS was worth it and the pain I felt after Kevin disappeared and blocked me from his life was the catalyst for my ministry and passion as a love coach and matchmaker.

I found me and love with a man that exceeds what I could have ever imagined. Thich Nhat Hanh is correct, love didn't leave, it only changed its form and enlarged itself in me, and here I am UNLEASHED from darkness and the invisible chains.

Step 7: Unleash Her

Expansion Learning Exercise:

Put a check by the part of Your BLISS is blocking you from experiencing the amazing love and happiness you desire?

_ Beauty

-Love

-Intuition

-Sensuality

-Significance

What is your plan of action to remove the block and unleash The READY WOMAN in you?

1. The first step in removing my blocks is

____

____

____

____

2. Removing this / these blocks will allow me the freedom to do the following

____

____

3. Signs and experiences that the block(s) have been removed are

____

____

____

____

4. RATE YOUR BLISS (Rate your bliss each day so that you are aware of how you're feeling and the types of experiences you may draw to you.) When you can feel happiness and bliss 10 consecutive days, you are on your way to creating amazing love and real happiness and all the magical experiences that come with it.

Today I am feeling/ Behaving

Day 1

Bliss ______ Happy ________ Bored ________ Angry _________

Sad ________

Day 2

Bliss ______ Happy ________ Bored ________ Angry _________

Sad ________

Day 3

Bliss ______ Happy ________ Bored ________ Angry _________

Sad ________

Day 4

Bliss ______ Happy ________ Bored ________ Angry _________

Sad ________

Day 5

Bliss ______ Happy ________ Bored ________ Angry _________

Sad ________

Day 6

Bliss ______ Happy ________ Bored ________ Angry _________

Sad ________

Day 7

Bliss ______ Happy ________ Bored ________ Angry _________

Sad ________

Day 8

Bliss ______ Happy ________ Bored ________ Angry _________

Sad ________

Day 9

Bliss ______ Happy ________ Bored ________ Angry _________

Sad ________

Day 10

Bliss ______ Happy ________ Bored ________ Angry _________

Sad ________

Chapter 8
Activate Your Bliss

Soulfirmation:

"Love is not just an amazing companionship, it's a legacy and a new way of living and believing. That's what makes it extra-ordinary"

Bliss Makes Love Flow & Dreams Real

Recognizing love is simple when you understand the love of Good. Good shows you the way but the way leads to bliss. Good knows when you're filled with optimism and love is inevitable. I understand now that bliss is God and God is Good and all of that lives in me. For that reason, all the other things I need and desire are added to me as necessary.

When you understand Good and have developed your bond and spiritual connectedness, there is a feeling you get. That feeling is Bliss and that feeling is the same feeling you will have when you meet "THE ONE". That's how you know you've met the one because bliss will tell you. When you know yourself, you will know if the relationship you are in is the relationship that is an amazing reflection of Good.

Love is not an abusive, demeaning or cruel. You do NOT have to be a doormat to have love. You don't have to tolerate being disrespected. You don't have to dim your light or quiet yourself down to have love. Love makes you more of what you are in the purest and most purposefully divine way. Love is not supposed to hurt physically or mentally.

Love is not sex! Love is clearly spelled out in I Corinthians 13:4-8. I will just put emphasis on verses 4 and 5: Love is patient, love is kind; It does not envy, it does not boast, it is not proud; It is not rude, it is not self-seeking, it is not easily angered, it keeps no record of wrongs.

I can truly say that love is contagious if you allow yourself to experience it. My husband loves me from a deep, right soul, level place and it feels so good that I can't help but give him the same love in return. We are the mirror to each other's soul.

I was celibate for one year prior to meeting my husband because I wanted to be single which means whole, not alone. Single means whole in body and soul. During my season of singleness, while preparing to be a wife who would prove to be pleasurable, soft and home for the right man, I trained myself to communicate through words and observe the actions of men to determine if they were good for me.

When sex is out of the equation, it's a lot easier to think soberly, and true motives are illuminated. Being sexually active makes it hard to make decisions from your higher good. You can possibly get lost in a fear-based thought pattern, feeling like you should do whatever it takes to keep the person. That person may not be the person for you but sex keeps you bonded and blind to the truth and to invisible chains.

Please remember, single sisters and brothers that a real emotionally healthy man desires to be a husband and build a home for his wife. A real emotionally healthy woman desires to be a wife and create the atmosphere for the home to thrive. Don't subscribe to playing house by living together. Assume ownership, legalize your commitment. Make your legacy a legal and binding document! Wives have legal rights not girlfriends.

New Script, New Name

Changing the theme of your life doesn't only encompass embracing your personal power and releasing the old programming; it is showing people how to treat you. This is called creating your bliss code. Your personal bliss code -is comprised of your values, your strong beliefs, your standards.

Your personal bliss code is your ability to remain authentic, peaceful and a way to protect your identity, heart and soul from unnecessary people and situations.

When we were enslaved to our past programming, we were constantly reminded of who we were and often that we did not matter by the way people treated us and what they said about us. In fact, a lot of the things they said became self-fulfilling prophecies for us, because a great deal of us had carried out their words. They said we were stupid, so we did stupid things. They said we were promiscuous, so we did promiscuous things.

They said we wouldn't amount to anything, so no matter what we accomplished, we were still unhappy. They said we would never find anyone better than them, and many of us still connect with the very people in our lives who give us the most rejection. Whatever they call out, we do a great job of answering to. After all, when you are a slave, you do as you are told until you understand the power you have to break the chains of bondage by knowing and owning your personal bliss code which holds your true identity, power and purpose. The key to your bliss code is in your name.

What Is Your Name?

Intuitively, names hold the mystery to our destiny. What you answer to gives foresight into who you believe yourself to be. Your slave name may have been fear, critical, not enough, pain, rejection, abandonment, lonely, broke, poor, bitch, whore, greedy, gold digger, low self-worth, low self-esteem, bastard, dog, dumb ass, stupid, irresponsible, inadequate. Those are the names we answered to, however, those names will be of no use to you in Bliss. The necessary step to activate your bliss is understanding the power of what we call ourselves and allow others to call us.

Harriet Tubman's birth name was Araminta Ross, but in her lifetime her name changed on three different occasions as she began to own her bliss. During her first change she became Harriet Tubman, when she started freeing other slaves by working the

Underground Railroad, she became known as Moses. Her name changed again when she instructed troops in the Civil War when her comrades began calling her General Tubman.

I began to understand the power of destiny within our names when I had my second child. Her father explained to me that in his culture, it is the tradition for the elders of the family to name a newborn baby within seven days after birth. They pray to God about the child's destiny for Him to reveal what the child should behold and become. You may have seen this is the film ROOTS when the character Kunta Kinte continued the tradition from his African tribe to name the child based on an intended destiny and then dedicated that destiny to God by lifting the baby to the sky and chanting the Arabic blessing. Well folks that's real and I got to experience its full power.

In the Yoruba culture of Nigeria, West Africa, when they agree on a name, they then have a naming ceremony on the seventh day to acknowledge and celebrate the arrival of the child and its destiny. I realized that this was a very important tradition to which he and I agree to participate. I was so afraid that I would not be able to pronounce my baby's name, but I trusted her father and I trusted Good.

By the third day after my baby's birth, my ex-husband's father called us with her name: Islamyaat Ayomikun Omodele. Islamyaat means "peaceful woman", Ayomikun means her "joy is full", and Omodele means "child remember to come home". When we call her, she answers to being a woman of peace, a woman whose joy is always full and she will always remember and be bonded to Africa. The fear of not being able to say her name disappeared because I couldn't think of a more fitting and glorious name for a child of a new generation, born free of invisible chains.

This name confirmed that my little girl would not experience what I had to go through to get to where I am today.

Your name is a special identifier that allows others to know and understand you, and hopefully be affected by you in a positive, uplifting way. The foundation of your destiny is in your name. Your life is in your name. What is your name? What is the one thing in your life you know you have been called to do? Every time you say "yes" to your name, you are saying "yes" to your destiny, provided you know the meaning of your name. So, what is it going to be, Goddess, Joy, Power, Love, Heavenly, or Confidence? What are you identifying with as your new name and ultimately the new theme of your life?

Call Me Nasira

When I got married, my husband (Boyo) renamed me Nasira which means glowing star in Arabic. Boyo named me that because he says I glow like a star and people are addicted to my healing rays of power. Those qualities bring him joy. Rewriting the new script for my life is so fitting to include a new name. It is a sign that the destiny to which I am called, is being fulfilled.

When God got ready to use people mightily during biblical times, there was a significant pattern He employed to signify that they were free from their past struggles and former way of living. Once they learned the lesson behind their struggles, they were elevated to becoming world changers. God changed their names so they would not be identified by who they once were, but by what they were about to accomplish and where they were going. For example, Abram was changed to Abraham, Sarai was changed to Sarah, Jacob was changed to Israel, Simon Peter was changed to Peter and Saul was changed to Paul.

I researched my name and discovered that it wasn't just a couple of cute-sounding words put together. Nekisha is South African in origin, although the spelling is slightly different. It means a woman of beauty. Michelle is derived from the masculine version of Michael, which means like God, so when you put the two together and call my name, you are referring to me as a beautiful woman who is like God.

It is now very important to me that people not only call me Nekisha, but that they say my whole name, which reminds me to be a woman of beauty inside and out and to demonstrate the character of Good that I have become awakened to. I am no longer Kee-Kee, Kee or whatever people feel like calling me. I am Nekisha Michelle, because it is very important to me that I answer to my full calling. And the more I hear my proper name being called, the more I will be reminded of that fact and remain accountable to my destiny and my purpose.

After acknowledging and taking ownership of the power of my name, I redesigned my business and my life to reflect and be in alignment with my purpose and bliss. The name of my company, "Nekisha Michelle International", is a beautiful place where you will experience God. It is the parent company of *Ultimate Match Agency, The Love Doyenne and Make Me A Wife Academy & Club.*

Noteworthy Name Changes
:

These are names of noteworthy individuals who are remembered because of their character and significance. Malcom Little to Malcom X; Rhonda Eva Harris to Iyanla Vanzant; Leroi Jones to Amiri Baraka; Stokely Carmichael to Kwame Ture, to name a few people whose individual purposes caused them to shed their birth names.

It makes a lot of sense why our youth change their names in hip hop or gang culture. They rename themselves based on what they want others to see. They are being renamed based on who they are and the characteristics they display. Even though some of the names are very shallow, the idea is the same. They want to identify with their new lifestyle.

As a ***Ready Woman***, what lifestyle would you like to identify as your own? What is your calling? What is Good calling you to do and how does Good want you to magnify your presence and significance? What is the new theme of your life representing? What is your new name? Genesis 32:27-30 states: The man asked him, "What is your name?" "Jacob," he answered. Then the man said, "Your name will no longer be Jacob, but Israel, because you have struggled with God and with men and have overcome." Jacob said, "Please tell me your name." But he replied, "Why do you ask my name?" Then he blessed him there. So, Jacob called the place Peniel, saying, "It is because I saw God face to face, and yet my life was spared."

Expansion Exercise:

In this space you have the luxury of rewriting your script for your new amazing love and amazing life.

1. What was the old story of your life?
2. What is the new script for the new story?
3. What is your bliss code to keep you intimate with Good?

I am Nasira Nekisha Michelle, the glowing star and beautiful woman who is like God. Please send me a message on Instagram **@thereadywoman** telling me who you are. Your name is

____

Now you shall be called OR share the meaning of your current

name here. ___________________________

1. What power does your new name or understanding of your birth name hold?

2. How will you be faithful in demonstrating the new theme of your life?

Let's Have Some Fun:

Now that you have a new name and new theme for your life, why not send out some fancy or fun announcements, much like we do with a newborn. Take a great picture and attach it to your new name. Send it out to your family and associates, announcing and declaring your new name and the new theme of your life

A. How do you think doing that will make you feel?

B. What type of presence are you creating with your new name and theme of your life?

The more you hear your new name, the more you will live it!

Resources for name searches: http://www.kabalarians.com/index.cfm

The Name Book by Dorothy Astoria

Digest of Muslim Names by Fatimah Suzanne Al-Jafari The Public Library.s

Chapter 9

Follow Your Bliss

Soulfirmation:

"To gain I must let go and when I let go, I allow more love, happiness, health and freedom than I have ever experienced or manifested before."

Bliss Grit & God

One day, I was on my way to training to renew my social worker's license. The training was located quite a distance from where I lived and I couldn't get anyone to drive me there because I didn't have a car. I called the travel hotline for directions and I later learned that they didn't tell me I'd have to take a two-mile country walk to reach my destination. The bus driver looked at me strangely when I told him where I needed to go. He wished me good luck and told me where to catch the bus back to the city in case I didn't make it.

Being in a strange environment made me feel uneasy. I began singing all my favorite songs to take my mind off of my fears. I was sweating, my feet were hurting, and as far as I could see, I hadn't gotten any closer to the hotel where the training was being held. I took a good look at my surroundings and decided to turn around and go back to the bus stop. It started to rain and I was very sad and frustrated, but I heard bliss say, "If you keep going, your destination is on the other side of that overpass." Bliss also said that if I made it to the hotel, I'd know someone there and they'd make sure I got home safely.

Because I learned to trust my Bliss rather than my fears, I kept going without further hesitation. I approached the overpass in less than five minutes and, sure enough, the hotel was right there in front of me! I started crying and singing and praising Good. This lesson showed me that we must never give up and go back to what was comfortable because what we desire is many times a five-minute walk away. And just as Bliss had said, I was given a lift home by a co-worker who was also in the training session. Bliss is real and it has a voice. The voice is there to guide us onto the right path for our lives. That path leads to greater fulfillment and greater responsibility, which is to make sure that after we realize our own bliss, to help others find it, too.

Joshua 1:15 states: "...until the Lord gives them rest, as He has done for you, and until they too have taken possession of the land that The Lord your God is giving them. After that you may go back and occupy your own land, which Moses the servant of The Lord gave you east of the Jordan toward the sunrise. I can't fully enjoy my freedom unless I am leading others to the place where I dwell in my heart and mind." Once you have experienced the pain of a broken heart, a broken dream, or a broken relationship, it is hard to watch others go through the same thing.

Now I am called to be one of the voices of reason and wisdom to help you on this journey from struggle to sparkle with habitual success. My calling is to help others see the 23rd Psalm manifest in their lives as it has in mine. This was the prescription my doctor failed to prescribe. It is not easy and that is why so many stop short of getting it all. This path takes Bliss, Grit & God.

Bliss Has an Image

To see who we truly are, separating from the bondage we once knew, should be learned, and how we used to see ourselves should be unlearned. This has a direct effect on how we will carry ourselves in our new life of bliss. Sometimes when we look in the mirror, we don't see a change, even though we are not who we used to be. Sometimes we take our slave clothes to our place of freedom out of comfort and just because we don't know anything other than those garments.

One day, I had an enlightening conversation with my business partner, and we were discussing how important image is to someone who is self-employed and working toward building an empire. I realized for the first time that I was literally still wearing my slave garments.

I finally understood why I didn't feel confident when I was among other professionals and why I was intimidated to sell my products and services to high end clientele. My image was not congruent to who I believed I was and where I was going.

After that conversation, I sought out a woman named Donna Dabbs from Cleveland, Ohio, to teach me how to create my new image. When you don't know what to do, you must find the people who do and learn what they must teach you. When freedom calls, doing things the way you've been used to doing them won't work.

During my initial consultation with Donna, I saw that she really knew what she was doing. She asked me several questions about what I wanted people to see when they looked at me without knowing or conversing with me. She then went through my entire wardrobe to see if theWre were any items that matched what I said I wanted. In a matter of twenty minutes, three closets full of clothes became one small closet that had the potential to give me the look that represented the new me. Finally, Donna confronted me with a critical question.

She asked me why I was hiding behind all the long skirts, blouses, pants, and jackets that hid my figure. To put it plainly, my clothes were boring and lacked character. And I didn't wear accessories—not even a watch. Why was I wearing clothes that made me look like an old church mother, rather than a young, energetic woman in her early thirties? I'm sure we all know the answer to that question: they were my low self-esteem clothes, left behind from the chains.

Donna was wonderful in guiding and helping me make wiser choices with my wardrobe. She even challenged me to buy tasteful clothing for making trips to the grocery store and even for lounging. Since working with Donna, my self-image has boosted my confidence and my ability to go after the high-powered clients, and I feel so good about myself each time I look in the full-length mirror she urged me to purchase. I also learned to take advantage of the complimentary makeovers at various cosmetic counters. I used to go to them whenever I had important meetings, or wanted to change my look a little or even drastically. It felt so good when people stopped to tell me how good I looked. When they saw Nekisha Michelle, they saw a confident woman improving her image from head to toe and inside out.

When I was in bondage, what I looked like didn't matter, if I was presentable. I was too confused and ignorant to understand or care. But now that I am in bliss, I want to look radiant and own my Goddess power and authority. Bliss has an image indeed, and that image is radiating the new me. I use this concept in my work with women. I teach skincare and makeup tips and I always say in class that it is important to look good, because when you look good, you feel good.

Bliss Loves Discipline

Bliss is the ability to improve the quality of your life. Ever since I entered Bliss, the quality of my life has improved with each passing day. For example, I've lost weight and I've gotten so much better at managing my finances, which has increased my wealth. Like many who struggle with their weight, I've been on every diet and have swallowed every kind of pill and mixed all types of powder. But knowing what I know now, I realized that I couldn't get rid of the weight or conquer any challenge until I filled the part of me that was deficient. Even though we know that having a weight issue, just like any other issue, can be the result of DNA, overcoming it depends on having a satisfied soul. When your soul is damaged, your heart broken, and your mind anxious, it is almost impossible to release unnecessary entrapments such as overeating.

A while back, I decided to go to a nutritionist and a therapist to help me see what I wasn't seeing in terms of not being able to lose weight and keep it off. The nutritionist told me that I didn't have the correct knowledge on what the body needs for fuel. She also went into detail about the importance of having regular bowl movements. She told me that my food portions were too big. She showed me a picture of what my plate should look like when I sat down to eat. I now realized that I had been eating way too much meat, not enough vegetables, and too many carbohydrates, or starches as we often call them.

And like a lot of us, I picked up my bad eating habits during my childhood. In fact, I used to cook the way my mother and grandmother showed me. I prepared meals that were filling and didn't cost a lot of money to make. I do understand that living in poverty and having a lot of mouths to feed puts good nutrition on the backburner, and keeping everybody from going hungry is the top priority.

I had to unlearn the poverty-conscious kind of cooking and use cookbooks and online recipes to make sure my plate looked like the model my nutritionist provided for me. Saying that I didn't know how to fix healthy food was no longer an option. I invested in a program that prepackages my food and delivers it to my home. All I should do is stick the food in the microwave or add some water to it. It saves me a ton of money because I no longer eat out, except for on special occasions. I also no longer have the stress of counting calories or worrying about portion control.

My therapist was also very helpful. She gave me homework, which consisted of writing in a sensations journal. She wanted me to track my feelings at least five times a day and write down what I did because of my feelings. What I immediately discovered was that I had no under- standing of the difference between being full and being satisfied.

As far as my eating was concerned, they meant the same thing. I would eat and eat because I didn't like the feeling of emptiness. I wanted to feel stuffed. And there was a direct link to my emotional life as well.

I was covering—or stuffing—my negative and anxious feelings with food. Whenever I felt empty, I would feel the strong emotions that stayed bottled up inside me. I knew I had to find another outlet for these strong emotions, and I had to learn to not surpass satisfaction each time I ate. I soon changed my diet and began eating lots of vegetables and drinking water. My appetite started to naturally decrease and the pounds began to leave me. When I was stuffed to capacity and ripping and running or catching a plane here and there to go and train or coach at one event or another, I thought I was okay.

I thought that having no room for anything else meant satisfaction. That is also why, when I became pregnant and then gave birth to my baby girl, I was sad, bored, and disappointed all the time. My life had changed drastically, and I wanted my full life back. I wasn't happy with not having a lot to do. I now know that satisfied is the place where I should live and being full is dangerous. This was proven each time I'd get on the scale or every time I went up to the next dress size. I can't say enough how much I love my simple life... and I am indeed satisfied.

Instead of forcing myself to reach goals that I can't perceive, I've start listening to my body and it is happiest in a 16W to 18W. Seeing you at one of my events or some appearance as a 16 or 18W, is now my focus. It's about doing and being what makes you feel good. At what size do you feel your best? Your second step should be to get there by force or by fire, don't sell yourself short on reaching your goals. Each time you do reach a goal, you add fuel to your bliss.

Exercise

Fitness expert, Carl Harmon, says, "Exercise is the most natural way to cleanse your mind and emotions. When your emotions are flustered and your mind cluttered, you will find refreshment after a good workout. When done correctly, it is only during exercise that your mind actually rests." I also read somewhere that "Health is your relationship with your body." I've found a non-traditional way to deal with the emotions that can sometimes be trapped called dance. It is a fun and energetic way for me to exercise and fuel my soul. I really enjoy Zumba, Hip Hop, Pole Dance and all forms of exotic dance. It makes me feel sexy, sensual and feminine. Not to mention it strengthens the core and it wasn't until I practiced these dances that I realized the power of my woman essence that makes my man crave me.

Money Habits

I filed bankruptcy at twenty-six years old. I learned my money habits from my parents and I spent money based on how I felt. Money, much like the food, was comforting to me. However, it was like I had holes in my pocket. Whatever monthly expenses I had left over went to eating at upscale restaurants and shopping. I lived from paycheck to paycheck and didn't know the meaning of saving. I was the queen of overdrawn bank accounts.

When I began a new way of handling my finances, I had to think back to how I learned about money. I realized that my father never had any, even though he worked the same job most of his adult life. When I was just a young girl, he would show me his pay stub and all the child support he owed. After that and taxes, he would only have about a hundred dollars or less per week. My mother was even worse than my father. She could never stay employed.

She bounced around from job to job and created financial crises for my grandparents to bail her out of, on a regular basis. Additionally, both of my parents filed bankruptcy at different times in their lives. My father even once jokingly told me that he files for bankruptcy every seven years.

When I started working, as a teenager, another interesting dynamic set in with my mother. She'd borrow my money and when I would ask for it back, she would say that she paid me back with the food I ate or the clothes she had bought me. Every time I would bring home money, she would find a way to take it; without fail. So, in my adult life, every time I would bring home money, someone would take it and I would create a crisis which always led to my friends having to rescue me.

Deuteronomy 28:1-14 discusses the blessings of The Lord if you are obedient to His word. Some of the blessings I am learning to receive are being the head and not the tail, being above and not beneath, and being the lender and not the borrower. I am working very hard to correct my perception and consciousness about my money.

My sorority sister, Lilly, is a financial advisor who helped me find ways to pay off my debt and start saving money. When I reach a specific amount, she will take me to a whole new level of investing. In the meantime, I've enrolled in a financial program at my church, and I am constantly reading books on how wealthy people think and act. One book that totally changed my perspective is Glenda Bridgeforth's ***Girl, Get Your Money Straight!*** One day at a time, I am learning to divide my income into several categories and assign money to these different areas. I practice tithing by giving a tenth and more to the church. I pay myself and after that is all taken care of, I live off what is left over.

My inspiration has been one of my girlfriends, who has also been my guardian angel. She worked so hard for many years, day and night, and now she has her own title company. She is also involved in various other areas of business that bring her additional streams of income. She is a single parent who put herself through college, got an MBA, built her house, and owns several cars. She attends church regularly, pays her tithes, and lives a Godly life. She is just in her early thirties. And she, too, fell on financial hard times at one point in her life, but she broke those chains and she is now my inspiration to continue to break through mine.

It was so affirming to see my girlfriend Clarissa Foster break her financial chains and challenge me to do the same. It would have been another story if I didn't know her, but because I do, it makes me so proud. Witnessing her 360-degree turnaround was so amazing, and it added fuel to my belief that if she do it, I can, too! In fact, I am grateful to her for instructing me on how to purchase my first house and how to take care of it when I was a single woman. Adapting to anything new doesn't happen overnight, but it can be done one day at a time with steady focus, practice and support and honoring your bliss.

Bliss Elevates You

When I'm in my element or in the right lane of my journey through life, there is a twinkle in my eye, and whatever I do causes me to stand out. Others see that glow and are attracted to it. We must all find our element so that we can shine. Shining gives us that well-deserved, positive attention and recognition that we all need to have a good dose of every so often.

I didn't start off as a successful business owner of my own dating and matchmaking agency. I started in network marketing or MLM back in 2002. The skills I learned there took me to the higher heights as I eventually excelled living in Los Angeles as the Director of Child Adoptions for a non-profit community agency.

Building someone else's dream tired me out and that is when I realized the energy and wisdom I used to pass audits and increase profits were transferable into re-energizing Nekisha Michelle International.

The creative power I was giving to others, helped to elevate me when I learned to do it for myself. But I owe it all to my humble beginnings when I was let go of my third Social Work position due to layoffs, I had only $100.00 in my bank account. At the encouragement of my mentor Debrena Jackson Gandy to take complete control of my financial future, I became a consultant in a direct sales company formerly Warm Spirit, investing $98.00 of that $100.

Saying yes to the home-based business opportunity was a scary investment into myself was the leap of faith allowed me to replace my lost income and gave me the liberty to do what I wanted, when I wanted. I was accomplishing my goals by working only 40 hours or less per month. In addition, what I learned was the more you grew on the inside, the more your money grew.

That is when I realized that working full time in Social Work was not the answer for me and I wanted to retire as a legacy builder of an enterprise. I have received so much more for, a job well done, apart from the financial gain. I could get the recognition that working for someone else never gave me. I remember being recognized as a Shining Star. That is when the top performers see their names in lights. It made me feel so good when I saw my name in lights among the top consultants of the company.

Too often we work so hard, doing things we really don't want to do and don't get recognized for either. We feel unappreciated and unnoticed. No matter what others might say, I have learned that everyone—whether they admit it or not— wants to be recognized and made to feel like they matter.

Although, I am no longer in direct sales, I own my own international company, it is the power of knowing that my light, my sparkle, my radiance, my bliss stands like a lighthouse and all the lost ships of women and men all over the world find me and allow me to use my wisdom to brighten their path. It's true that when you've found your bliss, it doesn't feel like work, is work, it is a delight and a pleasure to serve.

It is important to learn how to have a lot of fun. When I first became a consultant, I had never owned a business before, and I had never spent a day in business school; I had a serious fear of failure. But once I hosted my first few home-spa parties, I knew with practice and consistency that I could really do well. The most important thing was showing hundreds of women how to do well in entrepreneurship. As a result, I witnessed an overflow of self-esteem and confidence.

We took over the whole state of Ohio with top sales and the highest income earners in our area. I was having so much fun. I met new people, traveled to different places, shared my ideas, built a team, and challenged myself to be better and do more. At the end of the day, it didn't feel like work because I was having fun with what I was doing. I had fun at the pampering parties, the sales conferences, and even at the regional meetings.

I often heard that if you can do something for free, then that is what you are meant to be doing. To this day I was meant to be an entrepreneur and I have the drive to continue to grow and teach others the same liberties and gifts that come with ownership and bliss. From live events to my retreats all of it elevates my whole soul by increasing my fun factor while I service others.

The fun I was having got me my first to write-ups in two major magazine publications; Empowering Women and Black Enterprise Magazine. Since that time, I have been written about or given my advice in the best of them. That's BLISS in action. Before owning my own business, after working on a job for about six months, I noticed that I was always bored and unhappy. I loathed getting up early in the mornings and I didn't like getting off late in the evenings.

I was tired of being laid off, passed over for promotions, and putting all my eggs in one basket, only to see them crushed. I was tired of feeding other people's egos and keeping quiet to keep my light and personality hidden. This went on for ten years in the traditional social work practice that I thought I was bound to because I had degrees and a student loan of ninety-five thousand dollars to prove it. Over time, I realized that I wasn't in my element, and it showed, because all my light and excitement for life was being drained from me.

I was so serious all the time. My life basically consisted of walking a fine line at work for fear of being fired. Taking a risk to follow our bliss is worth it, because the longer you neglect your passion and what excites you, the longer you will feel unfulfilled, emotionally empty and lacking confidence.

Keep Your Life Fun

To keep your life fun and exciting, you must do things that are fun and exciting, no matter what your age. Think back to your childhood and what you liked to do or wanted to learn, and make plans to do them. It is never too late. Until you do the things that make you happy and make you feel satisfied, you will always feel like something is missing.

I am renewing my commitment to the girl in me. As I stated earlier, I have always liked to dance and I am dancing. I love the water and I am swimming. I love to be pampered and feel good, and I indulge in the best restaurants and stimulating, sisterhood conversations. In fact, my husband and I relocated to Atlanta to increase our fun and expand our income opportunities. I make fun fit into my schedule regularly. Now we share our time between Los Angeles, Atlanta and Lagos Nigeria.

You are a love diamond and all love diamonds are meant to sparkle. Others can find their way when you are sparkling and doing what you are supposed to be doing. When you are happy and joyful, others will want to be around you because of your light. The husband you have been waiting on will come when you start sparkling. The right job you have been waiting on will come when you start sparkling. The renewed sexier relationship that you have been praying for will come when you start sparkling.

The baby you have been waiting to have will come when you start sparkling. You must get in your element and your element will cause you to elevate and sparkle. I don't care what you went to school to do or what others may think of you, find your element and when you do, your light will be infectious. Sparkle love diamond, sparkle. You were created to sparkle with bliss. Fun equates to living and you're not fully living until you are following your bliss.

A Ready Woman Can Influence the Hurt

The most unforgettable moment when I knew that I was following my bliss, came after speaking for a Women's Day church function. A majority of my biological family was in attendance. It was a beautiful day and what I had to say was the focus. I spoke about how to access the power to bring about a new season/theme in one's life. One of the steps was about renewing the mind. Romans 12:2 states: "Do not conform any longer to the patterns of this world, but be transformed by the renewing of your mind.

Then you will be able to test and approve what God's will is-His good, pleasing and perfect will." New International Version (NIV). Leaving the old world and stepping into a new one that yields the results of soul harmony, happiness, and love to have the life that you can love was the basis of my speech. And not too long after, I found out that my blissful redesigned life was causing others to have the confidence to follow their bliss.

I received an unexpected phone call from my father. He called to tell me he loved me and that he knew I was called to teach and help our family break the habits that were keeping us lacking progress and fulfillment. He also shared with me that I helped him in so many ways mentally, emotionally and spiritually by delivering my talk during the Women's Day program. He said, "baby girl, I can't stop thinking about it."

He said he had begun to meditate on the process to which I provided and act to renewing his mind, and that it was helping him let go of the anger he had against Mama Maggie. My father said to me, "Thank you." In that moment, I realized part of my bliss was to teach my father that his true nature is to heal, love and live his bliss.

That meant forgiveness had to be a major demonstration in his life. It also taught me everyone has a story and sometimes we are a part of a story that doesn't always begin well but it works together for our Good and with Good. My father said that his only prayer is for all his children to know each other and we did.
As for my mother, I learned her anger and frustration was not because she hated me, but because she was frustrated, scared and angry with her life. My job is to love her regardless while living by my personal bliss code. You'll see her here and there cheering and taking all the glory for my transformation, growth and age defying looks.

My grandparents are so very proud and at this moment, I am working on retiring my grandfather and buying his hair salon so he and Mama J can enjoy their last years in plenty and peace.

Both of my brothers are doing extraordinarily well, one is a hip-hop rapper by night and social worker by day. My youngest we call him Mr. President because he is a big boss over at a top 10 major university.

My father passed away April 7, 2010 the day after my television debut following my bliss as a Relationship Expert on Los Angeles, top-rated KTLA-5 news.

We are all GOOD!

She's Ready Now

Sometimes we know what we want to do, but we need permission and confirmation that it is time to do it. A wonderful woman and executive coach, author and orator, Gail Blanke, was speaking for the opening of the Houston chapter of the National Association for Female Executives (NAFE). Gail gave a smooth, yet power-filled, classy speech on stepping into your power. She was promoting her book, Flying Between Trapezes. The one thing she said that struck a chord for me was that we all become afraid of the journey from leaving one trapeze to catching the next, but **"how good could you make it?"**

You could hear a pin drop in the room. Tears were rolling down my face because I knew I had done the necessary work on myself and others as a coach and transformational change agent to release this book and it was time to follow my intuition to make my life as significant as possible.

That was a turning point in my life, the moment when you know you've come too far and there is no more turning back. I got to sit and listen to the best fifty-minute speech ever and as a special gift of Good, I won a sixty- minute private coaching session with Gail.

When the time came for my session came, Gail coached me as if I had paid her thousands of dollars. That was a sign of royalty and the VIP status that following your bliss brings. It was time for me to soar at a higher altitude and touch not just my local market, but the world with the Ready Woman message.

I am now moving forward with Bliss and Good as the new companions of my RIGHT SOUL, while standing on the shoulders of my life coach AJ Johnson who constantly reminds me to keep my crown from falling off by honoring my spirit work and that it is not okay to reach my goals and it is not okay to not work toward my being better. AJ is an example of the type of people we need in our life to keep us accountable to what we say we want and being true representatives of Good.

I didn't get here by myself, I am here because of my dedication to me and a host of women that follow their bliss. Their sparkle has helped me to do the same. Gail Blanke, Rhonda Byrne, Glenda Bridgeforth, Delores Pressley, Connie Atkins, Dr. Valda Hilton, Amilia Wiley, Minnie Woodard, Clotilda Taylor, Oprah, Tyra, Dr. Belinda Scott, Lue McCain, Maggie Ardister, Mary Myers, Dr. Maya Angelou, Iyanla Vanzant, Jewel Diamond Taylor, Ethel Hedgeman Lyle, Nadine

Thompson, Judith Warren, Patrina Hughes, Dr. Shantel Thomas, Donita Jackson, Mary Kay Ash, Coretta Scott King, Debrena Jackson Gandy, Gloria Mayfield Banks, Clarissa Foster, Bettie Simpson, Tiffany Somerville, Sherry Fields, Marian Smith, Sharon

Tinsley, Claudia Guinther, Earlene Dulla, Koach Candye, Harriet Tubman, Vernetta Cox Dupree, Fantasia Barrino, Jennifer Hudson, Dr. Christine Diggs, Joy Donnell, Okera Banks, Sharon Gardner, Loni Love, Spirit, Kym Whitley, Madeline "Maddy" Jones, Queen Latifah and so many other awesome women who have believed in me or guided me to the right path, directly or indirectly.

In the words of Oprah, *"I come as one but I stand as many…"*.
I am **The Ready Woman**, a woman who turns her challenges and problems into a platform for love, income and influence.

Step 9: Follow Your B.L.I.S.S.

Expansion Learning Assignment:

1. Which lack of discipline in your life is keeping you from a state of bliss?

2. Create your plan to keep bliss active and strong in your life. The more bliss the more you attract the life you want.

3. How do you know the difference between bliss, happiness, boredom and depression and where do you believe you spend the most time?

4. In which ways do you feel like you have matured in wisdom since reading this book?

Your Ready Woman Review

The 9 Steps to Bounce Back from Adversity, Redesign Your Life for Amazing Love & Real Happiness.

Step 1: *Acknowledge the Nightmare*

Step 2: *Align Your Soul*

Step 3: *Reboot Your Spirit*

Step 4: *Rewrite Your Story*

Step 5: *Detox Your Life*

Step 6: *Feel Your Power*

Step 7: *Unleash Her*

Step 8: *Activate Your B.L.I.S.S.*

Step 9: *Follow Your B.L.I.S.S.*

Final Notes...

The Ready Woman book is only the beginning of filling your life with BLISS. I urge you to continue your transformation and commitment to being your own version of the Ready Woman by adding Nekisha Michelle on Instagram @thereadywoman . Instagram will keep you up-to-date with her products, services, events and more.

Work with the Plus -Size Love Doyenne & Matchmaker

Helping you bounce back from the disappointment of adversity, mastering self-love, and finding your life partner is what I do. If you're ready for a fantastic life and amazing love, you're in the right place. I've been turning frowns upside down since 2006. I can't stop and won't stop until I have helped you too!

http://www.ultimatematchagency.co/

Imagine where you could be this time next year.!

About the Author:

Nekisha Michelle Kee, MSW, Is the world's most beloved Plus-Size Love Doyenne, Matchmaker, and owner of **Ultimate Match Agency.**

Nekisha has been in everything from Ebony, Black Enterprise, Upscale, Rolling Out, Success, Plus Model Magazine, to being a TV Personality on OWN and HGTV. Nekisha Michelle is a former contributor to Huff Post.

Nekisha-Michelle redesigned her life after being a social worker and in non-profit administration for over 16 years to share her story and passion for finding real love for herself as a plus-size woman using BLISS. She believes everyone can be happy and have fantastic love. "Understanding it is not about color, shape or size but having the right state of mind."

Nekisha is a lady of Alpha Kappa Alpha Sorority, Inc. and received her bachelor degree from Virginia State University **(HBCU)** and a Masters of Social Work in 1999 from the University of Cincinnati. Nekisha Michelle carries a powerful, inspiring voice, engaging personality, and passion for helping others create an amazing life.

Nekisha resides in Atlanta, GA, and Los Angeles CA and is married to Boyo Agboola and is the mother of Ce-Ce and Izzy. *The author of The Ready Woman, How to Bounce Back from Adversity, Redesign Your Life for Amazing Love and Real Happiness. As well as Diary of a Ready Woman.*

Nekisha Michelle Kee is available:

Empowerment Speaker / Trainer
Press & Media Opportunities
Success Coach/ Consultant

For all other inquiries contact:

Nekisha Michelle International

1372 Peachtree Street NE
2nd Floor
Atlanta, GA 30136
Support@Nekisha-Michelle.com
Phone 1 (323) 596-1722

THE SEQUEL

To be a Ready Woman it takes Bliss, Grit and God and in the sequel book, Diary of A Ready Woman, you will be exposed to more women who used Bliss, Grit and God to transform their challenges and problems in income and influence. This next level is compiled by Nekisha Michelle Kee and co-authored by 12 fearless women. To follow their journey and be a part of the discussion www.facebook.com/groups/diaryofareadywoman

Order the Diary of a Ready Woman, www.diaryofareadywoman.org

READY WOMAN PUBLISHING & MEDIA
DIARY OF A READY
WOMAN
I Don't Look Like What I've Been Through Because
We're here!
READY WOMAN SOCIETY
#iamareadywoman

Join the Shift in Online Dating...

Dearest Friend:

You are so deserving of love and I want to do everything in my power to assist you on your journey. As you know I a serve as a love advocate that thinks out of the box. I am an avid supporter of connecting and dating online and would like to introduce to the ultimate, dating-for-marriage website, MarriageMindedOnly.com.

This is the only website and app that strictly, maintains an environment for serious dating to nuptials, globally. Upon joining, prepare to experience commitment-related interactions with like-minded individuals who seek long-term companionship and/or marriage, just like you!

XOXO,

Website: www.ultimatematchagency.co

VISIT THE READY WOMAN ONLINE STORE
WWW.SQUAREUP.COM/STORE/READYWOMANBOUTIQUE

@theReadyWoman

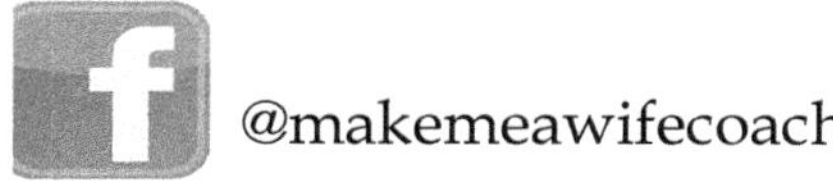
@makemeawifecoach

@nekishamichelle

Support@Nekisha-Michelle.com

THANK YOU FOR READING
THE READY WOMAN...
ARE YOU READY NOW?

www.ingramcontent.com/pod-product-compliance
Lightning Source LLC
Chambersburg PA
CBHW051904090426
42811CB00003B/454

* 9 7 8 0 9 7 0 7 1 7 5 0 4 *